A GUIDE TO

Style
&
Mechanics

Neil Daniel
Texas Christian University

A GUIDE TO

Style

&

Mechanics

Harcourt Brace Jovanovich College Publishers
Fort Worth   Philadelphia   San Diego   New York
Orlando   Austin   San Antonio
Toronto   Montreal   London   Sydney   Tokyo

Acquisitions Editor: Bill McLane
Manuscript Editor: Debbie Hardin
Production Editor: Kristina Sanfilippo
Designers: Frank Soley, James Hughes
Production Manager: Jacqui Parker

ISBN: 0-15-530329-5

Library of Congress Catalog Number: 91-72174

Printed in the United States of America

Contents

CHAPTER TWO
GUIDELINES FOR EDITING

CHAPTER THREE
PUNCTUATION

CHAPTER FIVE
ON WRITING AT THE COMPUTER

CORRECTIONS FOR THE EXERCISES

Preface

For years I have taught writing to college students and business executives and edited the work of other writers. As I have worked with my own writing and the writing of my colleagues and friends, I have kept track of the errors we make, the ways we allow our language to become inflated or clumsy or unclear.

Along the way I assembled a folder in which I gathered samples of the writing offenses I saw most often. On these loose pages I identified the principles of writing I thought were troublesome. I listed awkward sentences I encountered, and I tried to provide better ways of saying the same thing.

My early collection was typed on purple ditto masters that I duplicated over and over until they dimmed to invisibility. Later I entered the sentences and my corrections of them into a computer so that I could print them out fresh each semester. Some of my pages dealt with words: how to distinguish between *incidents, incidence,* and *instances,* any of which might show up in a context that required another. Some pages announced stylistic guidelines: avoid dangling and misplaced modifiers. Scattered through were other pages of punctuation rules: set off a nonrestrictive clause with commas.

This book brings system and organization to the material I have collected for years. I have made a distinction between guidelines for composing and guidelines for editing. Also, I have clustered punctuation principles and advice for avoiding sexist language apart from the sections on developing a tight, uncluttered style. I want to thank Bill McLane and other editors at Harcourt Brace Jovanovich for encouraging me to get the material together in this form, which I hope will be useful to others.

I want this book to be helpful to all writers—whether college students or professional writers, people who must write in their careers but who seem to have forgotten—or perhaps they never knew—the principles of clear writing. While I was in the middle of writing this book, I had a call from a lawyer whose firm had bogged down proofreading a statement of facts for an insurance case. Could I proofread their statement, they wondered; could I teach them where to put the commas? I read their statement of facts, and yes, they were in trouble. They needed no help in punctuating the ends of sentences. They knew better than I did how to cite and document cases to establish precedents. But their distribution of commas was capricious at best, sometimes fantastic. That weekend I wrote down the rules. I discovered to my surprise that if they knew only four rules for the placement of commas, they could solve their punctuation problems. Anyone can learn four rules! (You will find these rules on page 102.) The experience convinced me simple directions clearly stated would help many writers.

I want this book to be brief and readable, a guide useful to someone willing to work alone rather than a textbook requiring systematic instruction. I hope the guidelines I have included will get most writers through most writing situations and so establish a pattern that will lead to further editing precision. It is safe to offer this guarantee: any writer who masters the principles and guidelines in this book will see enough improvement and will learn enough about writing to go on learning and improving without additional help.

Readers familiar with other books on writing style will appreciate what I owe to authors who have pointed the way toward simplifying style. I didn't invent or discover the principles on which my guidelines are based. William Strunk, Jr. set the pattern, and when E. B. White revised Strunk's "little book," *The Elements of Style,* he prepared the way for many to follow. Joseph Williams at the University of Chicago has done more than any other authority to identify the offenses of institutional language, and in his book, *Style: Ten Lessons in Clarity and Grace,* he has offered efficient ways of combatting them. Richard Lanham's books on revising prose have taught us that a few rules, carefully applied, can take us most of the way out of the verbal tangle he calls "The Official Style."

This book is indebted to them all.

This book is indebted to my students as well, the weaker writers I have tried to help, often against their will, and the stronger writers who have sought help wherever they could find it. I owe thanks to those in my classes at the time I was writing this book. I asked them to respond to the material in draft form, and many of them did. Specifically, I want to thank Stephanie Reynolds, who not only read the book and commented on it thoughtfully, but actually used the book and became a better writer. She convinced me it works.

A number of colleagues from Texas Christian University read drafts of this book or provided copies for their students: David Cross in psychology, David Finn in marketing, Mildred Hogstel in the College of Nursing. I am especially grateful to Joe Law and Margaret-Rose Marek, who had their students use the book as a text and then asked the students to write out their reactions. The reactions provided a check on what made sense to the readers and what needed further clarification.

Other reviewers include Deborah Dietrich, California State University, Fullerton; Katherine Harris, Arizona State University; Dale Ross, Iowa State University; Linda Simon,

Harvard University; and David Wallace, Carnegie-Mellon University. I am grateful for their advice and help.

The most useful help came from Debbie Hardin, an editor's editor, who helped me prepare the final manuscript. Her good humor and her enthusiasm for the project kept me focused on the book, kept me eager to make corrections.

I thank Kristina Sanfilippo, James Hughes, and Jacqui Parker for their help in the production stages of the book.

Finally, I want to thank my wife Marcella, a professional writer who allows me to practice editing on her competent prose. She always thanks me graciously, but she doesn't always tell me whether she is following my advice.

I don't expect this book to be the final guide to composing and editing. I may improve on it some day; others surely will. This book began as a bundle of loose pages. In its present form it may appear still little more than a bundle. If it helps a few writers produce tighter, clearer prose, I will be satisfied.

—Neil Daniel

Introduction

You want to be a better writer. So do I.

Most of us who write every day or every week would like our writing to sound confident and to ring clear. We hope to avoid embarrassing errors. We look for help wherever we can find it.

Your library and your bookstore are full of books that will help—good books on writing that cover every aspect of the craft from how to discover ideas to ways of achieving a personal style to techniques of editing. No doubt you already have a dictionary and a thesaurus; you may have your favorite style manual to help you through forms of address and ticklish citations. I recommend such sources to anyone serious about writing. In the References section I include a list of the writing books I admire.

This guide will not improve on such books or displace them. It should, however, reach writers at a particular stage in their writing, students in college or office personnel who already know what they need to say and how to put their ideas together. This guide skips over such fundamentals as how to discover a workable topic or how to arrange ideas in their most persuasive order. It offers no advice on what constitutes an effective example. It concentrates instead on a stage of writing that for most of us comes somewhere in the middle of the process or toward the end, when the writer is crafting sentences or tinkering with them, striving for the most effective expression of ideas that are already in decent order. It provides suggestions about composing and editing that will help writers produce more readable texts and avoid the mistakes that most often clog and scramble beginning writing.

This book does not include rules for writing. The minute I say "rules" I risk being misinterpreted. The term might imply that good writing results from following the rules and avoiding errors. Nothing could be farther from the truth. Right and wrong, correct and incorrect, true and false are not useful ways of describing writing. Clear and readable writing results from a magic that cannot be reduced to a prescription.

Yet achieving direct and efficient communication depends on learning useful practices and avoiding the most common pitfalls. Most experts on writing agree about the characteristics of strong writing and the methods of making prose readable. The truth about good writing is that close attention to a few major principles will take us a long way toward the direct and personal style of writing that nearly all readers want.

The major principles can be presented as a limited set of guidelines. The purpose of this book is to present those guidelines simply and without adornment. I hope the guidelines are few enough and simple enough that they can be learned and mastered by anyone eager to write better.

In striving for a direct and uncluttered presentation of the guidelines, I have made statements that will strike some readers as dogmatic, inflexible. In the chapter on composing (Chapter One), for example, I have said, "Eliminate *very* and words like it." To illustrate, I have suggested that *I was discouraged* is a stronger statement than *I was extremely discouraged.* My students have objected, and one professional colleague blew his whistle. Come on, my colleague says to me, *discouraged* is not an absolute. It can be modified and strengthened with an adverb. This colleague and my students are right, of course, and I do not take the position that adverbs are out of place in clear, strong writing. Certainly there is no rule to that effect. Yet the principle remains valid, that avoiding intensifying modifiers will result in a leaner, stronger style. Illogically perhaps, I maintain the adjective *discouraged* is stronger without the adverb *extremely*.

What should a writer do who disagrees with me and wants to write *I was extremely discouraged*? Anyone who has read the guideline and has tried out the sentence in the form I have suggested is free to disregard the advice. This is why I prefer to call the recommendations guidelines instead of rules.

If you use this guide the way I hope you will, if you read the guidelines and practice using them, doing the exercises, trimming your own writing and adjusting your sentences with the guide at hand, you will gradually become alert to trouble spots the guidelines are intended to isolate. You will be aware every time you write a sentence with an empty verb and an abstract nominalization. In time and with practice, you will avoid a cumbersome statement even as it comes into your head. If that happens, we will both be happy.

In order to clarify the sense of the guidelines, from time to time I have used grammatical terms that may not be familiar to ordinary writers, writers who have not studied grammar since junior high school. I do so without apologizing. Terms like "subject" and "predicate," "non-restrictive modifier," and "finite verb" are essential in providing a context for the guidelines. Yet the guidelines are not intended to give lessons in grammar. Recent research has demonstrated convincingly that instruction and drill in grammar has little or no carry-over value in writing.[*] Moreover, most of us already know as much grammar as

---

[*] See Patrick Hartwell, *College English*, 47 (1985): 105–127. This is the only footnote citation in this book. Generally I mention important reference works in the body of my text in brackets. Those seeking the sources of my claims are urged to consult the References section at the back of the book.

we need to know for writing even if we don't have a grammarian's vocabulary.

At the end of the book is a glossary of technical terms that will help if the explanations are not clear. I have tried, however, to provide enough detail with each guideline so that the specialized language will explain itself. Some of the guidelines will not make easy reading, but there is no honest way to avoid technical details. My goal has been to make the guidelines useful enough to justify the concentration they require.

The two main chapters of this guide are "Guidelines for Composing" and "Guidelines for Editing." The distinction between these two parts is arbitrary. In general, the guidelines in Chapter One should be kept in mind early, while you are constructing sentences; those in Chapter Two are for when you are tinkering with the sentences, editing. As I suggest that difference, I am aware that it misrepresents the way we write. Most writers do not have a composing stage and an editing stage. We begin editing from the first word we write, and we are still composing as we complete the final draft. Or we may set both composing guidelines and editing guidelines aside during the early drafting of a report and save all conscious choices of wording and sentence structure until we have a substantial text in front of us. I won't presume to suggest a correct sequence for your writing or a right way to use this guide.

The arrangement of these two chapters, then, is a convenience. You'll find seven major guidelines in the first chapter, seven in the next. The presentation is stark: the guideline, a flawed example or two, corrections, and a brief explanation. Once you get into the guidelines, it's strictly business. Chapters Three and Four maintain the same spirit of efficiency. Chapter Three isolates the most useful guidelines for effective punctuation, and Chapter Four illustrates the most graceful ways of avoiding sexist language. Most writers must be conscious of punctuation and of selecting pronouns carefully both while they are composing and afterward, while they are editing.

The examples that illustrate the composing and editing problems are real, taken from published writing, institutional reports, and business communications. They are taken also from student papers at all levels, from first-year college composition through doctoral dissertations. I have not cited the sources. I mention them only to affirm that wordiness, excess formality, and occasional stylistic clumsiness show up in the work of competent, often practiced and professional, writers. We all make mistakes of the kind illustrated in this book. The challenge for each writer is to catch weak sentences either in the composing stage or in the editing stage. One advantage of writing over speaking is that we can go back later and edit. Before we send off a letter or a report, we can remove repeated words or change inflated phrases. A good writer is not a person who never makes mistakes but a person who corrects those mistakes before the document gets away.

I want to repeat that this book is a guide, not a set of rules. If you find that following a guideline would make your writing sound unnatural, ignore the guideline. For example, the guide suggests you avoid passive constructions. Yet in some situations the passive sounds right. If it sounds right, it probably is. In the final analysis, the best writing sounds natural. One purpose behind these guidelines is to help you train your ear so that crisp, tight prose will sound right. The other purpose is to encourage you to trust your own judgment.

Because it is a guide, you should not invest this book with more authority than it deserves. It was written for people in industry who regularly write reports and proposals, memos and business letters. They are counselors and architects, public administrators, surveyors, lawyers, and commercial artists—professionals who must communicate with clients and associates clearly and directly. It is intended for academic folk as well: students, teachers, and administrators who present themselves routinely in writing and want to make the best impression they can.

This is not a complete handbook of grammar and usage. I wouldn't want writers to give up their *Harbrace Handbook,* their style manuals, or their copies of *Fowler's Modern English Usage.* Nor is it a workbook for basic or remedial English. This guide is intended for writers of practical prose, willing to master a few simple guidelines, thankful to have a convenient reference beside them as they construct sentences or edit for correctness or worry over the rules of punctuation.

Emergency teams arriving on the scene of a disaster perform a sorting they call "triage." In one group they put those too severely injured to survive. In another group they put those who will recover without emergency aid. They concentrate their attention on those whose lives can be saved by medical help. The analogy is risky, but I think of the users of this book as those whose writing puts them in a middle group. Not severely crippled by writing problems, not fully competent without some aid, the users of this book need help in ready and usable form. I hope they will find it here.

Chapter One
Guidelines for Composing

SUMMARY ESSAY

When you read this chapter on composing, you will notice that it advocates a personal style, free of the institutional idiom we associate with official documents. The first sentence sets the tone: "The telltale weaknesses of bureaucratic prose are abstract nominalizations . . . and the passive voice." One of the guidelines (4) is "Prefer the more personal *you* and *I*." If you follow the guidelines carefully, your writing will shift away from the formal, academic prose you may have been taught to cultivate—impersonal and posing as objective.

You may wonder if this is wise advice. What if your chemistry professor has assigned a lab report and expects the narrative portion to be cast in the passive voice? What if your psychology teacher tells you never to refer to yourself in the first person when writing for her class? What if your supervisor at work says, "Be professional, not personal"? What if you are writing to the Internal Revenue Service!

The aim of this guide is not to contradict your instructor or your boss. But most professional scientists, when they are not writing for technical journals, refer to themselves as *I* or *we* and describe scientific investigation as if it were carried on by human beings. Stephen Jay Gould, among the premier science writers in America, deals with the clash of professional prose and a more readable popular style:

I have fiercely maintained one personal rule in all my so-called "popular" writing. (The word is admirable in its literal sense, but has been debased to mean simplified or adulterated for easy listening without effort in return.) I believe—as Gallileo did when he wrote his two greatest works as dialogues in Italian rather than didactic treatises in Latin, as Thomas Henry Huxley did when he composed his masterful prose free from jargon, as Darwin did when he published all his books for general audiences—that we can still have a genre of scientific books suitable for and accessible alike to professionals and interested laypeople. The concepts of science, in all their richness and ambiguity, can be presented without any compromise, without any simplification counting as distortion, in language accessible to all intelligent people. Words, of course, must be varied, if only to eliminate a jargon and phraseology that would mystify anyone outside the priesthood, but conceptual depth should not vary at all between professional publication and general exposition. I hope that this book can be read with profit both in seminars for graduate students and—if the movie stinks and you forgot your sleeping pills—on the businessman's special to Tokyo.

[Wonderful Life, p. 16]

I include this passage for two reasons. First, Gould recognizes that writing fretted with jargon is difficult to read. Second, Gould is fully at ease writing about his own process, referring to himself as *I*.

Another example may help to make my point. This is the beginning of an essay, "On Warts," by Lewis Thomas, a doctor handling a technical subject, but treating it informally.

Warts are wonderful structures. They can appear overnight on any part of the skin, like mushrooms on a damp lawn, full grown and splendid in the complexity of their architecture. Viewed in stained sections under a microscope, they are the most specialized of cellular arrangements, constructed as though for a purpose. They sit there like turreted mounds of dense, impenetrable horn, impregnable, designed for defense against the world outside.

In a sense, warts are both useful and essential, but not for us. As it turns out, the exuberant cells of a wart are the elaborate reproductive apparatus of a virus.

You might have thought from the looks of it that the cells infected by the wart virus were using this response as a ponderous way of defending themselves against the virus, maybe even a way of becoming more distasteful, but it is not so. The wart is what the virus truly wants; it can flourish only in cells undergoing precisely this kind of overgrowth. It is not a defense at all; it is an overwhelming welcome, an enthusiastic accommodation meeting the needs of more and more virus.

[The Medusa and the Snail, p. 61]

Lewis Thomas talks to his reader as he would talk to a friend.

Most authorities on business writing make a similar case for direct and personal communication, free of the institutional idiom just as good science communication is free of technical jargon. Perhaps the best modern expert on writing in business, Joseph Williams claims that one problem has afflicted generations of mature writers: "the problem of an unnecessarily complex prose style." [Style, p. 2]

A business letter need not be complex—nor distant nor formal. When E.B. White writes to a person he does not know to decline an invitation, he makes a conscious effort to be pleasant.

February 17, 1956

Dear Mr. Davison:

Thanks for your invitation to take part in the Forum program on humor. I can't do it, because I am incapable of making a speech.

I have known about this deficiency all my life but just this week I discovered, through X-ray examination, the true cause of it. There is a small exit called the "pylorus" leading from the stomach, and in me it closes tight at the slightest hint of trouble ahead—such as a speech, a platform, an audience, or a panel discussion. It closes and it stays closed, awaiting a turn of events that suggests smoother going. A man with a tightly shut pylorus is in real trouble and should be in a hospital, not a forum.

So I must beg off, as I always do when it comes to speech making. But I am grateful to you for the chance and I am sorry I have to miss the occasion.

Sincerely yours,

E. B. White

White is colloquial, saying, "I must beg off." He is gracious, thanking Mr. Davison for the compliment of the invitation. Yet he is firm, leaving no suggestion that he wants further urging.

An example from a writer who is not a professional essayist may offer a more realistic example. Here is a letter from the chair of a college English department, addressed to the dean.

To Dean Walton Etheridge

2 September 1992

Dear Dean Etheridge:

At the moment, the English Department is bleeding: Richard Crenshaw is dead, Ellen Overstreet is in the final year of a non-tenurable appointment, and Doug Wilson is hospitalized, with his return to the department questionable at best.

We are weakened, yes; but we have a first-rate opportunity to take the initiative in rejuvenating the department if only we're allowed to.

You've already given me the go-ahead to search for a replacement for Richard Crenshaw, and I assume we'll be allowed to replace Ellen Overstreet. Since the search machinery is in place, why can't we go on to search for a replacement for Doug Wilson?

I urge you to support this request, and I stand ready to deal with any questions you may have. Give us a chance to act by design rather than by reaction.

Yours sincerely,

Anne Loomis, Chair

Although the setting is a university, the occasion formal, and the request somewhat delicate, the writer has not retreated into abstract or impersonal language. The opening metaphor, "the department is bleeding," is calculated to get the dean's attention. Good writing, even in formal situations, gets the reader's attention.

The cause of much of the stiff, impersonal prose that hobbles business communications is the mistaken sense that a specific idiom distinguishes business letters from ordinary communications. The perceived idiom is distinguished by passive constructions and few references to the writer or the person written. Some phrases seem standard: "Enclosed please find," or "Please remit your payment in the amount of. . . ." An inexperienced writer may find security in formulas: if others have said it that way, then it must be okay. Besides, when the person at the receiving end of the letter reads, "Per your contract," that person will know this is a business letter, not a casual note. The trouble is, the reader may assume that because it is a business letter, it can't mean anything personal to the one receiving it. Suddenly communication is interrupted.

One more real world example will illustrate the communications block. This is a letter from a bank to a customer, explaining how a note is to be repaid.

Mr. David A. Weir
4915 Eighth Avenue
Fort Worth, Texas 76109

Ref: Loan #2315719-73

Dear Mr. Weir:

Enclosed please find coupon payment book on the above referenced loan.

In compliance with the terms of your Note and Deed of Trust monthly installments of $83.75 will be due and payable beginning February 12, 1992, with a like installment due on the 12th day of each succeeding month thereafter until yearly adjustment date.

On February 12 of each year your loan rate and payment will be adjusted and a new coupon book will be forwarded to you.

Should you have any questions concerning this matter, please do not hesitate to call.

Very truly yours,

Joanna Cable

The end of this letter suggests, whether sincerely or not, that its writer wants to be helpful. But the style of the letter, particularly the mention of "the above referenced loan," tells Mr. Weir that this is a form letter, probably one of hundreds sent every month, and the bank has no personal interest in him. The letter was written on a programmed typewriter or computer using coded stops to allow specific numbers and dates to be entered. It would be just as simple for the letter to begin, "With this letter is your coupon payment book for loan #2315719-73." And the third paragraph could say, "On February 12 of each year we will adjust your loan rate and payment, and we will send you a new coupon book." It doesn't take much to make a form letter sound personal to the person receiving it.

Let me offer a rule of thumb: if it sounds like a business letter—or a typical report or a term paper—it could probably be better. Try rewriting, following the guidelines in this chapter.

At the same time, I would urge you to avoid self-conscious mannerisms that often masquerade as personal concern or enthusiasm. Here I quote from a bulk mailing to the membership of a large credit union:

Read the exciting folder I'm sending along. Notice the benefits! This is ideal for EVERY MEMBER. Thousands of fellow members have already purchased this family security program.

The marketing director who wrote the passage wanted to convey personal concern for the membership. No doubt the letter is sincere, not simply a strategy to sell insurance. But when the writer says, "This is ideal for EVERY MEMBER," we must wonder. Instead of coming across as thoughtful and concerned, the writer sounds like a snake-oil merchant making a pitch from the back of a wagon.

Personal writing is not easy to master. Finding the simple, direct way of making a statement is more difficult than learning a set of patterns to cover typical situations. But as you work with the guidelines in this chapter, practice them, master them, clarity and directness—the hallmarks of a personal style—will come easier and easier. And as you take the time to think through each sentence and eliminate the official-sounding prose, you will restore your relationship with your audience and your language.

GUIDELINES

1. Find the true subject and correct verb.

The telltale weaknesses of bureaucratic prose are **abstract nominalizations*** (nouns made from verbs) and the **passive voice.** Consider this sentence in a consulting firm's proposal:

> Assistance is given in the formulation of a case statement outlining the history, background, goals, and financial objectives of the agency.

Later in the proposal, the firm writes:

*Terms set in boldface type are explained in the Glossary.

> *A pre-campaign survey is conducted and then an evaluation of the financial potential is made.*

The impersonal and institutional sound of these sentences stems mainly from the nominalized verbs: *assistance* derived from *assist; formulation* from *formulate* or *form; evaluation* from *evaluate.* The sentences can be improved simply by eliminating the nouns made from verbs and by stating clearly who is responsible for the action the firm describes:

> *We help you write a case statement outlining your history, background, goals, and financial objectives.*

For the latter sentence the firm could say,

> *We conduct a pre-campaign survey and then evaluate the financial potential of the target population.*

To give writing a personal flavor it is best to eliminate the signals of official or bureaucratic style. Decide what action the sentence is about and who or what performs the action (the doer or agent).

1a.   Eliminate nominalizations.

Example: *The builder makes an adjustment of his estimate to reflect the alteration in the plans.*

Correction: *The builder adjusts his estimate to reflect the change in the plans.*

Explanation: The important change here is from *makes an adjustment* to *adjusts.* One benefit of this correction is that the sentence is shortened. The more important benefit is that the abstract nominalization, *adjustment*, is converted to an active verb, *adjusts*, with no change in meaning and a noticeable improvement in directness. The other change, *alteration* to *change*, does not fit the guideline about nominalizations. But the simpler word conveys the same meaning in more natural language. Good writing always sounds natural.

> Example: *Since the charge to the committee was to look at both physical and fiscal needs, the decision was made to build an in-depth meeting around each area.*

> Correction: *Charged to look at both physical and fiscal needs, the committee decided to devote one meeting to each set of needs.*

Explanation: Several corrections have been made. The most important of the changes is from *the decision was made* to *the committee decided*. The sentence is stronger because the abstract noun, made from a verb, has been converted to an active verb. The passive form, *was made*, has been eliminated. Elimination of passive verbs will be covered in the next section.

In a related change, the initial abstract noun, *charge*, has been put in verb form, *was charged*. Although this change introduces a passive construction, in violation of 1b., the sentence is improved. Who charged the committee is of minor importance in this context. The focus is on deciding to devote one meeting to each set of needs. The passive, therefore, is not damaging.

Eliminating the jargonistic modifier *in-depth* is part of the attempt to eliminate the bureaucratic tone. Changing the abstract *area* to the more concrete *set of needs* makes the statement more direct.

As you compose, be alert for clues that will help you spot abstract nominalizations. Notice that the following phrases, each containing an empty, generalized verb and a noun made from a verb, can be reduced to a single direct verb:

PHRASE	VERB
conduct an assessment	*assess*
do an examination	*examine*
make a correction	*correct*
perform an adjustment	*adjust*
take a count	*count*
give a performance of	*perform*

One signal of nouns made from verbs is that they are often introduced by abstract, all-purpose verbs like *make* or *do*. Another is that the noun form is likely to end in *-tion, -ment, -ance, -ence*. When you see such constructions, look for ways to revise them.

1b. Avoid the passive voice.

Example: *The search for properties that meet Techtron's investment criteria is aggressively conducted by staff members of Techtron, Inc.*

Correction: *Staff members of Techtron, Inc., aggressively search for properties that meet our investment criteria.*

Explanation: In addition to being more direct, the statement with the active verb puts the subject of the verb, those who search, in front of the verb. In most situations, this one included, who acts in the sentence is important and should be emphasized.

Notice in the following pairs of short sentences that removing the passive construction strengthens the sentence:

PASSIVE	ACTIVE
The criteria were determined by the board.	*The board determined the criteria.*
The cake was selected by the children.	*The children selected the cake.*
The pie was chosen by him.	*He chose the pie.*

Part of the strength of the second sentence in each pair is that the logical subject, the performer of the action, is placed directly in front of the verb.

Occasionally, the logical subject of an action, the performer, is not known or not important. For example, in this sentence,

> The stature and wisdom of the men and women who
> have given so much in this effort is unquestioned,

the compliment would be diminished by an effort to name the logical subject. Another example comes from the acknowledgments of an institutional report:

> The commission did its work in four committees: the
> educational committee was chaired by Malcolm
> Anderson; the admissions and financial aid committee
> was chaired by Evelyn Roach; the athletics committee
> was chaired by Lee Honna; and the fiscal resources
> committee was chaired by Solomon Brown.

The intention of this sentence is to organize the credit statement by committees, not by individual names. The logic of the acknowledgment would be hidden by putting the clauses in the active voice.

The point to be emphasized here is that the generalized guideline, *avoid the passive voice*, is only a guideline. You will write sentences in which the passive voice is appropriate. If so, keep the passive construction.

2.   Take noun phrases apart.

Trying to be concise and at the same time convey a great deal of information, some writers stack too many words together. Or they may produce convoluted chains that confuse more than they clarify. Consider this passage from an academic journal:

An assumption is always made, in the measurement of intelligence, that there are recognizable, quantifiable differences between children, even though the calculated proportion of environmental and genetic influences in the I.Q. are a matter of contention. The more recent developments which have taken place in the calculation of those proportions are mostly statistical reanalyses of old data on, for example, twin studies. Thus old measurement errors and the unconscious assumption of those times must also be a part of any reanalysis of intelligence measurement.

The ideas in this paragraph are not difficult. The passage says that if we reexamine the measurement of intelligence, I.Q., we must take into account the unconscious assumptions on which the older calculations were based. Taking noun phrases apart requires that we pay close attention to chains of prepositional phrases and strings of nouns.

2a.   Watch out for chains of prepositional phrases.

A series of **prepositional phrases** is clumsy for at least two reasons. One is that such a series is a form of repetition and is therefore stylistically flawed. Consider the following sentence:

The response to the publication of the report by the Chairman of the Board has been enthusiastic.

The sentence is not grammatically incorrect, but jerks along awkwardly. The sentence could be rewritten:

The report by the Chairman of the Board has received an enthusiastic response.

The other reason for regarding linked prepositional phrases with suspicion is that each phrase contains a noun, often an abstract noun, perhaps a nominalized verb. A string of prepositional phrases is therefore a warning sign that the writer needs to find a subject and verb and discover a more direct statement.

Example: *The young woman's fascination with science led to the selection of a number of courses in which the majority of her time was in the lab rather than the lecture hall.*

Correction: *The young woman's fascination with science led her to select courses that kept her in the lab more often than in the lecture hall.*

Alternate correction: *The young woman's fascination with science kept her in the lab more often than in the lecture hall.*

Explanation: The first correction is shorter than the original. The main improvement, however, results from trimming the abstract nouns and making the statement more direct. The second correction trims the sentence further. The second correction might be too lean for the writer's purposes.

2b.   Avoid strings of nouns.

Technical writing, in particular, often uses strings of nouns, lined up in complex compounds, to achieve economy. In an aircraft operating manual, one list of controls includes the following:

Afterburner fuel flow light

Afterburner nozzle control over-ride switch

Afterburner nozzle "open" position light

Fuel system shut-off valve

Fuel boost pump switch

No doubt a pilot could master the names with a little time and practice. If we disassemble *afterburner nozzle control over-ride switch,* we discover it refers to a switch that overrides the automatic control of the nozzle of the afterburner. Less densely packed, the phrase is still somewhat abstract, and it trails off in a pair of prepositional phrases. But it is more readable.

Let's look at another example.

Example: *High pressure compressor bleed air is used to perform engine service functions such as compressor inlet anti-icing and the cooling of internal parts that are subjected to extremely high temperatures.*

Correction: *Air bleeding from the high pressure compressor is used to de-ice the compressor inlet and to cool internal parts subjected to high temperatures.*

In technical writing it is not possible to eliminate scientific and technical language. The aircraft manual is not written for an eighth grade audience. But writing for a more general audience can be made readable, even if the content is technical. One example of readable technical material will illustrate. The following paragraph is from "The Panda's Thumb," in which Stephen Jay Gould explains the structure that allows pandas to strip bamboo stalks to get food.

The panda's "thumb" is not, anatomically, a finger at all. It is constructed from a bone called the radial sesamoid, normally a small component of the wrist. In pandas, the radial sesamoid is greatly enlarged and elongated until it almost equals the metapodial bones of the true digits in length. The radial sesamoid underlies a pad on the panda's forepaw; the five digits form

*the framework of another pad, the palmar. A shallow
furrow separates the two pads and serves as a channel-
way for bamboo stalks.*

[The Panda's Thumb, p. 22]

3.   Choose the most direct statement.

Some conventions of ordinary speech reduce the efficiency of written expression. The most conspicuous are
constructions with the **expletives** *there* and *it* and repeated
sentences with forms of *be*.

Example a: *Over the past few years there has been a gradual
increase in the percentage of female engineering students.*

Example b: *It is certain that these ideas will influence the
future course of our university.*

Example c: *She is a person who appreciates the challenge
of rigorous training.*

Notice that all these sentences can be trimmed for efficiency:

a. *Over the past few years the percentage of female engineering students has increased.*

b. *These ideas will certainly influence the future course of
our university.*

c. *She appreciates the challenge of rigorous training.*

More efficient, more direct writing is stronger writing.

3a.   Write away from *there* and *it*.

Example: *If there is a presence of hydrocarbons, the well is
completed and the necessary production equipment is
installed.*

Correction: *If hydrocarbons are present, the well is completed and the necessary equipment installed.*

Alternate correction: *If we find hydrocarbons, we complete
the well and install the necessary production equipment.*

Explanation: Notice that using *there* puts off the subject
of the action and often introduces a noun made from a
verb. The first correction leaves part of the sentence in the
passive voice; the second correction replaces the passive
construction with active verbs. Whether the alternate correction is appropriate depends on the situation. Sometimes
the logical subject of the verb need not be named (see 1b.).

Example: *It is for these reasons that committees central to
the organization are charged with review of the company's policies.*

Correction: *For these reasons, committees central to the
organization are charged to review the company's
policies.*

Explanation: Eliminating the construction with *it* has
not dramatically altered the sentence. But because the
noun *committees* is in the subject position, the statement is
more direct. I have also changed the noun *review* to a verb.
The rewritten sentence is shorter by four words. Eliminating words is not the goal here, but usually a shorter
sentence is more direct than a longer sentence.

3b. Be wary of forms of *be*.

Because the issue here is repeated use of *be* forms, not
single instances of *be*, this guideline must be illustrated
with a passage rather than a single sentence.

Example: *Where will financial aid funds come from? This was a fundamental question addressed by the committee. The committee wants to be certain that financial aid continues to be available at necessary levels for all students with financial need.*

Correction: *Where will financial aid funds come from? The committee addressed this fundamental question, hoping to guarantee financial aid at necessary levels for all students with financial need.*

Explanation: Rewriting this brief passage to reduce the number of *be* forms requires some changes that are desirable for other reasons. The passive construction has been eliminated in the second sentence. The phrase *be certain that* has been changed to the verb *guarantee*. The second and third sentences have been collapsed into one. The goal, of course, is directness. Forms of *be* are only a symptom that the style needs work.

4.   Prefer the more personal *you* and *I*.

Example: *Students will find the Activities Office open and friendly. All are encouraged to drop in at any time— between classes, on weekends, whenever you are free.*

Correction: *You will find the Activities Office open and friendly. You are encouraged to drop in at any time— between classes, on weekends, whenever you are free.*

Explanation: Aside from violating the principle of consistency, by shifting from the **third person** to the **second person**, the sample passage sends a mixed message. It speaks of friendliness, but treats students as impersonal referents. The corrected sentence incorporates the assumption that the primary readers are students and addresses them as *you*.

To reinforce this guideline I quote a brief passage from a doctoral dissertation on rhetoric:

> *After tracing the development of stasis theory through its amplification in the works of medieval rhetoricians, this work will return to examine the dialectic method of Plato. It will attempt to establish that Socrates was using stasis theory in the dialogues even though Plato never used the label.*

I would advise the candidate to write in the **first person**:

> *After tracing the development of stasis theory through its amplification in the works of medieval rhetoricians, I will return to examine the dialectic method of Plato. I hope to show that Socrates was using stasis theory in the dialogues even though Plato never used the label.*

While some academic writers argue that a dissertation should be impersonal and distant—formal, they would say—I disagree. And in the writing most of us do every day—office letters, memos, progress reports, even college papers—the personal tone established by referring to yourself as *I* is more persuasive than the artificial third-person style.

5. Use tense and person consistently.

Shifting from past **tense** to present without a good reason or drifting among the pronouns—from second **person** *you,* to third person *they,* to impersonal *one*—these inconsistencies mar the writing of many beginners.

Example a: *The office is in one of its busiest periods of the day, and suddenly the power shut off.*

Example b: *One must be able to communicate to an audience exactly what you want them to see or know.*

Each of these sentences is flawed by inattentiveness. A writer must learn to catch the shifts as they happen. Example a should be corrected to

> *The office was in one of its busiest periods of the day, and suddenly the power shut off.*

Of course the context might make it better to put both verbs in their present forms. Example b should read:

> *You must be able to communicate to an audience exactly what you want it to know.*

Here, too, the context would determine whether the pronouns should be second person, *you*, or the impersonal *one*. Some writers in some situations would be uncomfortable with the personal *you* and still want to avoid *one*. In that case a writer might say:

> *An engineer must be able to communicate to clients exactly what they need to know.*

5a.   In narrative or informative writing stick to present or past.

Example: *The Wife of Bath is the crowning achievement of Chaucer's ironic portraiture. Although she appeared confident, even brassy, in her discussion of her five marriages, there is no evidence that she had been unfaithful to any of the men she married.*

Correction: *The Wife of Bath is the crowning achievement of Chaucer's ironic portraiture. Although she appears confident, even brassy, in her discussion of her five marriages, there is no evidence that she has been unfaithful to any of the men she married.*

Explanation: A convention of literary criticism holds that works in print, though written in the past, exist in the present for their audience. It is customary, therefore, to write about literary characters using present verb forms. Whether present or past, however, the verb forms should be consistent. This passage about the Wife of Bath introduces a complication into the choice of tenses, for the matter of the story, in the literary present, includes information about the woman's past. For this reason, *appeared* must be made present, and *had been unfaithful* must be written in the past—but in the simple perfect form, not the past perfect, so that it is consistent with the evidence offered in the present.

5b. Avoid mixing *one* and *you* or *one* and *he*.

Example: *One has to know his own limitations. You can't just say, "I will," and expect to succeed at everything.*

Correction: *You have to know your limitations. You can't just say, "I will," and expect to succeed at everything.*

Alternate correction: *One has to know one's limitations. One can't just say, "I will," and expect to succeed at everything.*

Explanation: In general, as the next section will say, it is better to prefer the more personal *you* to the more abstract *one*. This is not a grammar rule, only a stylistic principle. But the grammar rule does hold that if you use *one*, you must refer to the same person as *one* later in the sentence. You can't switch from *me* to *he* or from *one* to *she.* On the choice between *one* and *you,* the only firm rule is that you must be consistent.

This guideline is best illustrated by an extended passage. The following sentences are taken from a book on career strategies. A good deal of the connecting material has been stripped away. But notice that the writer shifts, in a single paragraph, from the first person *we* to the third person *people/they,* to the impersonal *one,* to the second person *you.*

> *Whether we like it or not, all of us are part of some social environments. . . . In each situation we play a role—parent, child, boss, subordinate, or just a member. . . . Nevertheless, there is no denying the Pygmalion effect—that people try to live up to what they perceive as the expectations of others in the group to which they think they belong. . . . One's own values inevitably lead to the conclusion that in a free society people have a responsibility to more than just themselves. . . . Knowing, then, what others think you should do and caring about what others feel . . . are vital ingredients to the formulation of your career strategy.*

Whichever form this passage should take, whether it refers to the reader as *one* or addresses the reader as *you,* the passage should be consistent. Any sharp reader will notice if it is not.

6. Be careful with transitions.

Connecting words, often called **transition** words, lead a reader through the text. It is important to choose them carefully and to be conscious of the links they establish, whether of logical consequence, of time, of addition, of contrast, or of any other relation between ideas. Often the differences in meaning are difficult to put into words. But we ought to be conscious of them. To illustrate, *for* and *because* mean nearly the same thing when they are used as conjunctions. But notice we would say, *I came inside because it was raining.* We probably would not say, *I came inside for it was raining.* Moreover, while we often begin a sentence with a *because* clause—*Because my car wouldn't start, I had to ride the bus*—we almost never begin a sentence with *for* used as a conjunction. The correct transition word is justified by the intended relation between the thoughts being joined. *However* means something slightly different from *but; since* conveys a different relation between ideas than either *while* or *because.* Most of us are aware of these differences. We get in trouble if we are careless.

6a. Choose the right linking word.

Example: *The present system of reporting involves two extra steps, and I think we could save time by routing the reports directly from the receiving office to the department managers.*

Correction: *Because the present system of reporting involves two extra steps, I think we could save time by routing the reports directly from the receiving office to the department managers.*

Alternate correction: *Because the present system of reporting wastes two steps, we could save money by routing the reports directly from the receiving office to the department managers.*

Explanation: The causal connection between the ideas, and therefore the logic of changing the reporting system, is not conveyed by *and.* The first correction **subordinates** the first clause and indicates the relation of ideas with *because.* The alternate correction makes the sentence even stronger by using a stronger verb, *wastes.*

Another example will help to make the point. Consider the sentence,

> *On the other hand, since oily skin can persist into middle age, a strong cleanser may be too drying for older skin or for people with both dry and oily areas.*

The relation between the clauses is not accurately represented by *since.* The claim that a strong cleanser may be too drying for older skin does not depend logically on whether oily skin can persist into middle age. Here *and* would be the better choice:

> *On the other hand, oily skin can persist into middle age, and a strong cleanser may be too drying for older skin.*

Even better might be to separate the two clauses and treat them as independent sentences:

> *On the other hand, oily skin can persist into middle age. A strong cleanser may be too drying for older skin.*

The effect on people with both dry and oily areas, mentioned at the end of the original sentence, is a separate problem and deserves a separate sentence.

6b.   Place the transition word strategically.

Example: *Athletic programs have made a significant contribution to the university's past and have played a vital role in our present national stature. They too will contribute to our success in the decade to come.*

Correction: *Athletic programs have made a significant contribution to the university's past and have played a*

vital role in our present national stature. They will
contribute to our success in the decade to come as well.

Explanation: The connecting **adverb** *too* in the second
sentence is ambiguous. It can modify *they* (athletic programs) or *will contribute* or *in the decade to come.* We
remove the ambiguity by moving *too.* Once it is moved to
eliminate possible confusion, however, it doesn't seem to
be the best connecting word. *As well* sounds more natural.
The sentence might also be changed to eliminate the abstract nominatization *contribution,* following 1a. It would
then read as follows:

Athletic programs have contributed to the university's
past and to our present national stature. They will
contribute to our success in the coming decade as well.

7.   Trim your style.

The advice of William Strunk, captured in *The Elements*
of Style, by Strunk and White, is, "Omit needless words."
No one would quarrel with the wisdom of Strunk's advice,
but most of us are unsure how to follow it. Which words
are not needed? How can I cut out words that sound natural without converting my writing to a sterile outline? No
one can say in advance which words will be needed in a
passage of prose. But needless words often come in pre-
dictable types or follow recognizable patterns. The best
advice is to train yourself to spot the types of words and
the patterns that usually introduce unnecessary words.
Guidelines 7a. to 7e. should help.

7a.   Replace long words with simpler words.

Example: *This, of course, can lead to an inefficient and*
costly utilization of available academic resources.

Correction: *This, of course, can lead to inefficient use of academic resources.*

Explanation: The principal offender in this sentence is the inflated *utilization*, a long synonym for the simple *use*. Once the long word is replaced by a shorter word, the other changes seem natural: combining *inefficient* and *costly* and deleting *available*.

Example: *In an attempt to alleviate the problems caused by lack of definition, many emerging disciplines resort to the acquisition of a formula borrowed from a firmly established discipline, in hopes of investing their own area of study with greater legitimacy.*

Correction: *To correct their lack of definition and gain legitimacy, many emerging disciplines borrow a formula from an established discipline.*

Explanation: Removing abstract and elevated words like *alleviate* and *acquisition* simplifies the sentence. The writer is then able to see that the opening phrase, *In an attempt to alleviate . . .* and the closing phrase, *in hopes of investing . . .* are both reasons for borrowing a formula. The reasons can be brought together to make the sentence crisp.

Perhaps the best way to make the point that simple words are clearer and ultimately more impressive than longer, inflated words is to provide a brief list of common offenders. As you look at this list you will no doubt be reminded of other inflated words and phrases that can be replaced with their simpler equivalents.

INFLATED WORD OR PHRASE	SIMPLER EQUIVALENT
is contingent upon	depends on
initiate	begin
endeavor	try
is cognizant of	knows

utilize	*use*
deem	*judge*
prior to	*before*
subsequent to	*after*
transpire	*happen*
render	*give*
eventuality	*result*
transmit	*send*
remit	*send back*
perceive	*see*
ascertain	*find out*
pursuant to	*following*

7b.   Eliminate empty words.

This guideline is related to 7a. In both guidelines the principle at work is simplicity, the most direct statement of an idea. But in this instance the offending words are not inflated, only empty. We may write *the color green* when simply saying *green* would convey the idea. We may write *a stretch of highway twelve miles in length* when *a twelve-mile stretch of highway* would do.

> Example: *Drilling is a very risky business and usually not suitable for someone seeking income.*

> Correction: *Drilling is risky and usually not suitable for someone seeking income.*

Explanation: The first sentence is not wrong, simply longer than it needs to be. Whenever we can cut words without losing meaning, we improve the force of our writing. Notice that in the sentence above, four words, *a very risky business*, have been replaced by one, *risky*. Eliminating *very* will be covered in 7d.

A list of constructions that should be trimmed almost automatically will help to make the point. Pay attention to the pattern so that you can find similar phrases to trim in your own writing:

WORDY PHRASE	TRIMMED PHRASE
the fact that	*that*
the process of composition	*composing*
the act of demonstrating	*demonstrating*
the factor of size	*size*
the element of surprise	*surprise*
the concept of airiness	*airiness*

This list could be expanded almost indefinitely without ever being complete. You will develop your own list of favorite offenders as you practice trimming your own writing.

Another list could be made of pointless modifiers. These are words and phrases that creep into our speech almost unnoticed. In written language, however, they are intrusive.

Example: *The track is basically an oval twice as long as it is wide.*

Correction: *The track is an oval twice as long as it is wide.*

Example: *He stood listless at the counter, essentially with nothing to do.*

Correction: *He stood listless at the counter, with nothing to do.*

Example: *We have certain rules everybody must follow.*

Correction: *We have rules everybody must follow.*

This guideline covers such modifiers, usually unnecessary, as *actually, virtually, given, specific,* and many more. These words, of course, are not empty of meaning. As a writer you must decide when they contribute to your message and when they are simply filler. You should distinguish between the following uses of *different*:

We have identified six different varieties of oak trees on our land. (*Different* should be deleted.)

These varieties of oak trees are different from those found in Europe. (*Different* cannot be deleted.)

7c.   Prune circumlocutions and redundant pairs.

Although this guideline could be included with 7b., it covers a category of empty phrases that requires special attention. Included in this category are phrases like *each and every, any and all, willing and able, hope and trust.* Each of us has a repertoire of such phrases, entirely idiomatic, that pepper our informal speech. Indeed, because they are so conventional, so characteristic of speech, a writer may be tempted to use them to achieve a colloquial, informal style. But they are wasteful; they contribute to wordiness; they should be eliminated.

Example: *First and foremost, we must pick the proper register.*

Correction: *First we must pick the proper register.*

Example: *We have various and sundry reasons for preferring the full and complete line.*

Correction: *We have many (or several) reasons for preferring the complete line.*

The wordiness of the redundant pairs helps to make the point that achieving an informal, colloquial style requires more than simply writing as we talk.

Another set of phrases to trim includes not redundant pairs, but idiomatic circumlocutions:

Example: *During this period of time, Lee was treated by seven specialists.*

Correction: *During this period Lee was treated by seven specialists.*

Example: *Our engineers then proceeded to analyze the structural defects.*

Correction: *Our engineers then analyzed the structural defects.*

Keep in mind that *a point in time* is really *a time*. Work done *on a daily basis* is done *every day*. The list of such circumlocutions is nearly endless.

7d.   Eliminate *very* and words like it.

Nearly all **intensifying words** and **superlatives** can be eliminated without weakening the force of a sentence. *I was very eager to return* is weak compared with *I was eager to return. The committee was extremely disappointed* carries less force than *The committee was disappointed.* The paradox in this principle is related to the way we achieve strength in writing: the fewer words we use, the stronger the statement. Notice that a traffic sign that said, *Bring your car to a halt*, would not be as effective as the sign *STOP*.

Example: *I was extremely discouraged to learn that my extension had not been granted.*

Correction: *I was discouraged to learn that my extension had not been granted.*

This sentence could be strengthened even more:

I was discouraged to learn my extension was denied.

Example: *These last ten years have been very trying ones for me.*

Correction: *These last ten years have been trying for me.*

Explanation: The principle of using fewer words to strengthen a statement accounts for deleting *very* and for omitting the unnecessary *ones.*

7e. Cut out *who is, which are, that may be.*

This guideline covers nearly all **relative clauses, restrictive** and **nonrestrictive.** *The book that is on the table* should be rewritten *the book on the table. The clients who are waiting for your call* is more efficient as *The clients waiting for your call.*

Example: *Two additional lights will improve the safety of the space which is between the two dorms.*

Correction: *Two additional lights will improve the safety of the space between the dorms.*

Explanation: The important change in this pair is deleting *which is.* In addition, *two* has been eliminated because *between* implies that two dorms are involved.

Example: *Between the ages of one and seven, my son suffered from asthma which was of so critical a nature that it necessitated regular trips to the hospital emergency room.*

Correction: *Between one and seven, my son suffered from asthma so critical that it necessitated regular trips to the hospital emergency room.*

Explanation: The main improvement here is deleting *which was,* after *asthma.* Notice, however, that in correcting the sentence the writer has omitted *the ages of* and has reduced *of so critical a nature* to *so critical.* One improvement leads to another when you begin to trim your style.

EXERCISES

The exercises on the following pages are keyed to the guidelines provided in Chapter One. You will find it helpful to do the exercises as you work through the guidelines. If you try the exercises at a time when you are not studying the guidelines, you may want to refer to the guidelines to help you identify the needed corrections.

Most of the sentences in the exercises are taken from published sources or from papers written by advanced college students. Many contain no grammatical errors or flagrant stylistic blunders. They may sound fine to you. Yet most of the sentences or passages can be improved with careful application of the guidelines. The exercises are intended to provoke discussion. From time to time you may decide that making changes the guidelines seem to indicate will make a sentence more cumbersome rather than improve it. If you feel that way, you should resist the pressure to change it.

The solutions to problems (potential answers to the exercises) are presented on pages 153–231.

1.   Find the true subject and correct verb.

Directions: Rewrite the following sentences to eliminate nominalizations and avoid the passive voice. Make other corrections as needed to improve the clarity and directness of the sentences.

1. Advanced courses should be designed specifically to utilize and reinforce competencies (knowledge and skills) acquired in the completion of preliminary coursework.

2. This utilization may be achieved through the coordinated use of computers, research projects, and written assignments in the courses.

3. If the purchase is approved, final negotiations are completed, the purchase agreement is finalized, all remaining escrow contingencies are removed, and the title is transferred.

4. For its larger mission to be possible, it will be necessary for additional resources to be found and allocated to the college.

5. The decision about the choice of the right course of action was made by the night nurse, acting entirely on her own.

6. Data were collected concerning high school students' interest in engineering as well as the quality and types of applicants. In addition, current and projected enrollment and job demand information for engineering students were analyzed. Other programs were examined to determine the need for resources, including faculty, equipment, additional library holdings, facilities needs, etc. Questions concerning the impact of such a program on other programs, including residential living needs, were explored. Finally, estimated costs were gathered based on the experience of other universities.

7. Employees are required by company policy to report additional income earned by outside consulting.

8. Elimination of unneeded paper and unutilized forms can be achieved by judicious use of the paper shredder.

9. Reading stations are provided for examination of newly received materials prior to check-out.

10. This is an exaggeration on your part of the significance of the role of the new equipment.

11. Your contribution to our agency is appreciated.

12. Make an estimate of the amount of time spent by you before submitting your report.

13. If the cost is known, make an entry of the amount in the first column.

14. Analysis of the data is done by computer.

15. Recent expansion of the building has contributed to the easing of congestion in the corridors.

16. A survey of students was conducted to arrive at an estimate of the level of student use at peak hours.

2. Take noun phrases apart.

Directions: Rewrite the following sentences to eliminate cumbersome chains of prepositional phrases and strings of nouns. You may discover that other changes will improve the readability of the sentences.

1. The significance of observation to the practice of quality nursing care has been well documented in the literature. However, documentation of the role of observation in the development and subsequent implementation of research activities has been limited.

2. The library has a book of familiar quotations of famous authors.

3. The construction of a new wing of 9,000 sq. ft. on the east end of the building will contribute to the relief of congestion.

4. It is impossible to make an accurate estimate of the time of arrival of every vehicle in our fleet.

5. Every one of the solutions to this problem has at least one flaw.

6. The university's placement of a student into an agency for the purpose of field education brings a number of reciprocal responsibilities into action.

7. Design Inc. is a well respected Dallas-based graphics business consulting firm.

8. We have included our business client reference list and a current CDS annual report. We normally prepare a more comprehensive proposal or full-scale fund raising action plan but, due to your quick-reaction timing requirements, we have submitted this short term memo at your request. We would like the opportunity to meet with you to discuss the project in more detail and to respond with a more formalized document regarding our approach to your needs.

3. Choose the most direct statement.

Directions: Rewrite the following sentences to make them more direct.

1. By acquiring oil and gas properties only where wells have been in production for some time it is possible for our investors to obtain the benefits of owning valuable natural resources—oil and gas—without exposure to the significant risks of drilling.

2. In a recent survey it was revealed that 10% of graduating high school seniors are interested in a field of study we do not offer. This means that there is a group of at least 200,000 students that currently cannot consider our institution when selecting a college.

3. There is evidence that this lack of balance has had a negative effect on retention of upper-level females, and there is a feeling among some that it would be desirable to have a more balanced female/male ratio.

4. There is a high demand for engineers that will continue to grow for the future.

5. What are the forces that are responsible for the shifts in buying patterns? This is the question that pesters those in the industry who are charged with meeting consumer demand. While it is never possible to know what the causes are or what trends will prevail with certainty, it is a sure folly not to be aware of the patterns and not to try to anticipate the shifts.

6. There is a feeling among the employees that the new hours will improve company morale.

7. It is always difficult for me to write the first sentence.

8. Wherever there are oppressed citizens there is an unstable government.

9. We are the committee that decides which applicants will be on the final list.

10. The bulletin outlining the new guidelines will be in the workroom and will be available for anyone who is planning to request a leave.

11. In this corner there are the dictionaries and the other reference works that will be helpful to those who are preparing reports.

12. The new policy is that no one may smoke in the main lobby.

4. Prefer the more personal *you* and *I*.

Directions: The examples in this exercise are paragraphs rather than single sentences. Rewrite them to sound as if they were written to real people.

1. Within the next few days all staff members in your department should complete the enclosed personalized forms in order to report their earned and unused vacation time as well as their accumulated sick leave as of May 31, 1992. The form requests information in the detail which is required for the university's annual financial reports and for implementation of a new payroll system this summer.

Therefore, it is important that this office receive the information at an early date.

2. It would be difficult at this particular stage to even come close to telling you what the fee for the campaign itself would be. It will be based upon our findings, the geography in which the campaigns are to be conducted, the various kinds of program machinery that need to be set in order to assure that it will be a successful effort. Even though our fee is a flat fee and is not based upon a percentage, when a fee is looked at from a percentage viewpoint when the campaign is over, the percentages have run as low as five percent and as much as sixteen percent.

3. In the guide, typical writing problems are examined, and the cures for these problems are given through discussion and example. In many cases, options and alternatives are presented. An attempt is made, successfully it is hoped, to avoid direction by decree. Thus, the approach is more practical than academic. The aim of this guide is not to make writing more sophisticated (although it may become so) but to make it more direct, straightforward, and easy to follow and to help the writer develop a style that will reflect favorably on the work being reported or proposed.*

5. Use tense and person consistently.

Directions: Edit the following sentences to make them consistent in tense and person.

1. The confusion over this renewal raises the question of what our policy had been before the new regulations were enacted.

2. The employees are enjoying the refreshment center and have wondered what we did without it.

---

*I took this example from a style guide for technical writers.

3. Every student must have the work in on the day assigned. Don't be late.

4. One has to be familiar with the terrain before he can drive confidently.

5. Everyone should have your own copy of the employees' handbook. Employees should consult it for regulations regarding vacations, sick leave, and personal time as well as arranged leaves of absence. One can always get some time off if you need it.

6. Current openings are available on tape by calling the job list number. Anyone interested in a particular opening should go to the personnel office for an application form. Refer to the position by the code number on the job list included on the tape.

7. Career goals should incorporate more than one's salary and title.

6.   Be careful with transitions.

Directions: Rewrite the following sentences paying particular attention to the linking words. Transitional words should indicate the correct relation between ideas and should be placed to avoid ambiguity.

1. The artist of the work is Edvard Munch, a Norwegian, and the painting was done between the years 1904 and 1907.

2. This screening process typically eliminates between 90% to 95% of all submitted properties.

3. I hope you will take a close look at the opportunity offered by Roger Breen, and if there are any questions that I can answer, please feel free to call.

4. Thank you for your continued interest and we will look forward to receiving your signed agreement soon.

5. By maintaining stiff standards my high school

teacher was preparing me for college; although, I didn't appreciate it at the time.

6. We have published a new biography that also covers the early years.

7. Two new entrances have been opened on the west side of the building to ease congestion at peak hours. Employees will not be able to use these entrances during the early morning shift, however.

8. According to Freire, it seems as if he would like to totally change our concept of education completely.

9. The new spark plugs have a higher rating than the manual specifies, and thus you should use them only as a temporary solution.

10. It is not something that I do for anyone else, I continue education myself for my own benefit and satisfaction that I can accomplish what I set out to do.

11. The deadline for this report is not far off, and we need to get together soon.

12. The operator will add oil, so he needs to check the current level first.

7. Trim your style.

Directions: Revise the following sentences to eliminate inflated language.

1. Modification of this statement reflecting her observations to the form of a question provides greater direction in developing the remainder of the steps of the research process.

2. Experienced researchers, however, realize the conceptualization or development of the research question requires an ongoing literature review not only suggested by initial observation but also by the finalized question.

3. The preponderance of the more recent works have

neglected to consider the historical context of the economic theory in the initial stages of its development.

4. Having utilized this technique in many analogous situations, I am cognizant of the benefits as well as the attendant risks.

5. General Operating Instructions are supplemented by Specific Operating Instructions to which reference is necessary in order to operate an engine of a specific model and series. Specific Operating Instructions include specific procedures and information for a given engine series which may differ from that presented in the General Operating Instructions. Nevertheless, a working knowledge of the information presented in the General Operating Instructions is considered a necessary prerequisite to the use of the Specific Operating Instructions.

6. *Afterburner Nozzle Control Over-ride Switch*—Provision is made on some engines for a motor actuated, manually operated afterburner nozzle control over-ride. The afterburner nozzle control over-ride switch has two positions: OPEN and OFF. The over-ride will remain inoperative when the switch is in the OFF position. Should it be desirable for the pilot to select an "open" afterburner position during periods when the nozzle is normally closed, the over-ride switch may be moved to the OPEN position. This will cause the motor actuator to over-ride the nozzle control and hold the afterburner nozzle "open" as long as the switch remains in the OPEN position.

7. Please utilize the means of egress to the rear.

8. We must effect savings to the maximum extent possible.

9. The full range of potential applications of this program is difficult to conceptualize.

10. You may initiate the procedure whenever you deem it appropriate.

11. Subsequent to her arrival, the manager commenced her perusal of applications.

12. We will endeavor to secure the edition you have indicated on the request form.

13. Our compliance is contingent upon the timeliness of your reply.

14. Our agent will inform you regarding what transpires at the annual meeting.

7. Trim your style (additional exercises).

1. The following passage of bureaucratic prose uses the empty word *process* five times. You should be able to rewrite the passage to eliminate *process* entirely. You may want to suggest other changes to make the passage clearer and more direct.

> Last year the promotion committee prepared letters of inquiry for all those who had been through the promotion *process* during the previous five years. In general these people were asked to comment, in as much detail as they cared to, about their experience in the *process.* They were also invited to make evaluative comments about the *process* and to make recommendations, if they had any. The *process* of identifying those who should receive letters, distributing the letters, waiting for replies, and, finally, reading them was quite lengthy. That, plus the inability of the chair of the committee to continue the *process* toward the end of the year, is the reason that this year's committee has had to finish the project.

Rewrite the following sentences to eliminate extra words.

2. The initial review of the literature essentially consists of a thorough search of all available studies related, in general, to the identified research question.

3. A number of our members have written to express their frustration and disappointment with the fact that they are receiving multiple requests to join when they are already members.

4. Computer science, mathematics, and physics are areas that are fundamental to any program in engineering.

5. The fact that they perform well without the training does not mean they are performing at their maximum.

6. A major issue in the field of computer engineering is that of defining the nature of the discipline.

7. These engines employ a can-annular type combustion chamber with a number of separate combustion liners or burners.

8. We would be pleased for you to contact each and every one of our clients since we have had a happy relationship with each one.

9. When the objects of study are cells and tissues far removed from a living body, there is often no compelling reason to address social, political, or moral issues related to human beings.

10. We are definitely opposed to politicians who use their influence to amass wealth.

11. Our warranty provides full and complete coverage during the first ninety days.

12. I came home absolutely exhausted after my first day as a volunteer.

13. It is our professional opinion that a plan could be developed that would be within your $10,000 budget and that your goals could be reached within a 45-day time frame.

14. Homeowners who are developing a budget that will include home repairs face a task that is complicated.

15. The exhibit is displayed in a large room which contains the individual inventions which have contributed to the development of the computer.

16. The evaluation process is a continuing one and part of the teaching method. As such, it can be used as a device for helping the student to gain security and a sense of direction through increased recognition of the positive and negative aspects of his/her performance.

ON THE NUMBERING OF GUIDELINES

In the Introduction I have said the distinction between "Guidelines for Composing" and "Guidelines for Editing" is arbitrary. The arrangement of the guidelines is a convenience of the presentation, not a logical necessity. The separation between Chapter One and Chapter Two breaks the guidelines into readings of manageable size. To maintain the continuity between the chapters and to simplify referring to the guidelines, I have numbered the guidelines consecutively, from 1 through 7 in Chapter One, from 8 through 14 in Chapter Two. The main guidelines for style and mechanics are in these chapters.

When you get to Chapter Three and Chapter Four, you will find I have extended the sequence, starting with 15 in the chapter on punctuation and starting with 25 in the chapter on avoiding sexist language. The series ends with 30. The numbering is not intended to imply the relative importance of the guidelines.

As a teacher and writing coach, I believe this book gains in readability and usefulness from its limited number of guidelines. Many style manuals are forbidding because the number of rules is so high. The reader is daunted—so much to learn! I have trimmed all but the essentials. Surely anyone can master seven guidelines for composing. Next come seven for editing. I am convinced fourteen guidelines are enough to make a difference in your writing.

Chapter Two
Guidelines for Editing

SUMMARY ESSAY

The guidelines in this chapter, intended for the editing stage of your writing, present an assortment of strictures and advice. One way of distinguishing the recommendations in Chapter Two from those in Chapter One is that these guidelines are more nearly prescriptive rules. For example, guideline 8 says "Use singular verbs with single subjects, plural verbs with plural subjects." This is not avuncular advice; it is as close to a direct order as the flexibility of English grammar will admit.

The most revered modern book on writing is Strunk and White, *The Elements of Style*, mentioned in Chapter One. A charming feature of this book is that it presents the elements of style as commands. "Form the possessive singular of nouns by adding 's." "Omit needless words." Quoting these rules I am tempted to punctuate them with exclamation points. Although I admire the conviction of Strunk and White, I have suggested from the beginning of this guide that the conventions of edited English are too pliable and the demands of the academy or the market place are too various to claim there is only one right way.

I'll repeat here what I said in the introduction: good writing does not result from following the rules and avoiding errors. Yet a writer has no choice about making subjects and verbs agree in number. Dangling or misplaced modifiers will jump off the page and catch the sleeve of any alert reader. If you are careless about your pronouns, some reader is sure to sniff and say, "Good writers never use a reflexive pronoun for the subject."

Because the guidelines in this chapter are more prescriptive, more like rules, than the guidelines of the first chapter, I have called them editing guidelines. By this label I mean to capture an important principle about writing as a dynamic process. While you are composing a draft of a letter or a school paper, you can ignore the rules. You can let the words flow as easily as they will. If you are lucky and if the writing goes well, the ideas will tumble out on the page forming themselves as coherent collections of syntactic meaning, sentences mostly but not necessarily, gatherings of words in happy phrases. For many writers this sort of untrammeled flow, unconscious of correctness and conventions, is essential to fluent writing.

But before writing of this sort can be called good writing, before it is ready for others to read, it has to be patted into a sensible order, packaged intelligently, pruned perhaps—in other words, edited. At this stage good writers will listen carefully to their own reading, whether silently or aloud, will make judgments about the relations between sentences, and will pay attention to the conventions of edited American English. The writer may have produced well formed sentences at the first draft and because of long practice may have put commas in the right places. Some writers can do that. But even so, every good writer checks to be sure. For many writers a convenient checklist of rules or guidelines, a checklist based on the most common kinds of mistakes and carelessness is helpful. This chapter provides such a checklist.

Seven guidelines in all, this checklist may look like a hodgepodge. It includes some rules firmly grounded in the system of English grammar. It includes at least one guideline some writers would classify as a matter of style: "Keep coordinate elements in parallel form." One guideline deals with punctuation, and another directs your attention to spelling problems.

The apparent lack of system is a function of the way the guidelines were derived. Every writing expert has a different list of problems to attack, more or less tied to the errors writers make. A productive study of student errors was conducted in the late 1930s by John Hodges as he prepared the first edition of the *Harbrace Handbook* (1941). In 1983, Maxine Hairston asked friends and colleagues of various walks of life to rank a set of errors writers commonly make according to how grating the errors were. She published a list of the most offensive in *College English.* More recently, Robert Connors and Andrea Lunsford studied thousands of student papers and isolated the twenty errors most frequently committed by college students. The results of their study appeared in *College Composition and Communication,* 1988. Cataloguing errors, however, is not the purpose of this guide. Joseph Williams puts the issue of error into perspective. In his important book, *Style: Ten Lessons in Clarity and Grace,* Williams divides principles of usages into "rules and RULES." Separating real rules from nonrules and from optional rules, he offers a sane defense against the sniffery of so-called "purists." But he insists that some errors in usage, particularly egregious, will brand a writer as illiterate. It is useful to know that.

In the end, deciding what errors to include is a matter of taste. Even careful research in this slippery area is affected by the prejudices of the investigators. The same is true of my study and research. I have been collecting samples of student errors through a long career of teaching. I have examined and edited the correspondence of businesses—insurance companies, banks, social service agencies. The editing problems I have chosen to include as targets of these guidelines reflect my prejudices. They reflect my experience, as well. I believe that a writer who can follow these guidelines consistently can eliminate most of the editing problems writers encounter.

You may be surprised to discover, as you read the guidelines in this chapter, that the grammar is fairly simple. I have dealt with grammar head on, talking about subjects and modifiers, requiring you to deal with the difference between clauses and phrases. I still offer no apology for this direct approach. You will realize, once you get past the problem of what to call things, that you probably know all the grammar you need to write well. You have, after all, been speaking and writing intelligible sentences virtually all your life. A scholar's understanding of the subtleties of syntax is not necessary for writing. If it were, few of us would ever write.

Of course, the rules change some when you write a college paper or put your words on company stationery. But the main change comes from your realization that someone else, someone you may not know very well, will be reading your words. And because the words are in writing, not spoken, they will lie there on the page for the reader to see. Any mistake, from a simple typographical misprint to a glaring confusion of which word is the subject, will stay there to cause confusion or to invite scorn.

You know the grammar; you just have to be alert.

Editing for correctness and a direct style comes down to having a sharp eye. This is true for catching slips in the forms of pronouns; it is just as true for eliminating redundant modifiers. Each of us develops an eye for the right constructions by constant practice. You won't get it simply by reading through this guide. If you use this guide frequently and check your own writing against the guidelines again and again, you will find that your eye gets keener. You will catch the slips faster and more easily. By a curious paradox your improvement will not mean that you can relax or that you will spend less time rereading your work. In fact, the opposite will happen. For as your eye becomes more practiced, you will see more chances for improvement. You will develop discrimination, a taste for clean writing, and probably a list of additions to this simple collection of guidelines. Your attention to the demands of clear, concise, even elegant prose will never end.

GUIDELINES

8. Use singular verbs with single subjects, plural verbs with plural subjects.

One of the earliest acquired and most crucial of grammar rules, that **single subjects** take **single verbs, plural subjects** take **plural verbs,** requires no special instruction. Determining whether a subject is singular or plural, however, can be tricky when the number of the subject is obscured by surrounding words. Your ear may deceive you, or the logical topic of a sentence may not be the grammatical subject. If you get it wrong, no one will excuse you on the grounds that it was a tough call.

Example: *Everyone taking the class need their own copy of the manual.*

Example: *The impact of industrial chemicals and other pollutants are obvious along the river bank.*

Both of these sentences need correction. Although *everyone* seems to suggest many, it is grammatically a singular pronoun and requires the singular form of the verb, *needs.* The grammatical subject of the second sentence is *impact,* not *chemicals* or *pollutants.* Therefore the verb must be singular, *is.*

8a.   Indefinite pronouns are usually singular.

Example: *None of these solutions are practical.*

Correction: *None of these solutions is practical.*

Explanation: The subject of the sentence is the **pronoun,** *none,* not *solutions.* Because *solutions* is closer to the verb, a writer might miss the grammatical subject. Moreover, the writer might not be aware that *none* is necessarily singular. Notice that understanding the source of *none, no one,* makes the number clear. But most of us don't have time to think through or look up word derivations. The simplest way to deal with **indefinite pronouns,** nearly always grammatically singular, is to learn a representative list:

anything	*anyone*	*anybody*
everything	*everyone*	*everybody*
neither	*none*	*no one*
either	*someone*	*something*

The only common indefinite pronoun regarded as plural is *all. Any, some,* and *most* can be either singular or plural, depending on what they refer to. Referring to **mass nouns** such as *water* or *sand, any, some,* or *most* would take a singular verb. Referring to **count nouns,** such as *trees* or *books,* these indefinite pronouns would take plural verbs.

8b.   Don't be misled by prepositional phrases.

Example: *Volunteers come from the Rotary Club and Camp Fire. Their number of volunteer hours vary depending on the season.*

Correction: *Volunteers come from the Rotary Club and Camp Fire. The number of their volunteer hours varies depending on the season.*

Explanation: Because *hours* is next to *vary*, the writer has been misled and has used a plural verb. The grammatical subject, not necessarily the logical subject, is *number*. The singular *number* takes a singular verb. Notice that as we correct the sentence, we can see that *their* does not properly modify *number*. *Their* belongs with *hours* instead.

A related problem of subject-verb agreement is introduced when a sentence or clause begins with *there*, particularly if *there* is combined with *is* to form a contraction.

Example: *There's at least fifteen boxes in the back room.*

Correction: *There are at least fifteen boxes in the back room.*

Explanation: By the conventions of edited American English, the grammatical subject, postponed by *there*, is the noun phrase following the verb.

8c.   In compound subjects joined by *or* or *nor*, the nearest noun phrase governs the verb.

Example: *The executive officers or their delegate have the authority to override actions of this committee.*

Correction: *The executive officers or their delegate has the authority to override actions of this committee.*

Explanation: Even if the subject of this sentence were expanded to three compound elements—*The trustees, the executive officers, or their delegate*—the rule of agreement would still hold: the nearest **noun phrase** determines the number of the verb. But if an element introduced by *or* is in parentheses—*The executive officers (or their delegate)*—a convention of punctuation, that parenthetical elements are not part of the grammar of the surrounding sentence, would make the subject plural.

Example: *Neither the dancing master nor his students has listened to the bell.*

Correction: *Neither the dancing master nor his students have listened to the bell.*

Explanation: The rule for *nor* is the same as the rule for *or*.

9.   Avoid dangling and misplaced modifiers.

The general rule about modifiers, that they should be close to the words they modify, will not always prevent confusion. The most striking violations of good form associated with modifiers are **dangling modifiers** and **misplaced modifiers**.

Example a: *Unless otherwise instructed, the policy will be surrendered as of November 10.*

Example b: *The engine of this car is four cylinder, four stroke, and horizontally opposed in the rear.*

Both of these sentences are marred by confusing modifiers. The modifier in Example a is called a dangling modifier because *instructed* has nothing to modify. The opening phrase should be made into a clause, either *Unless we are instructed otherwise* or *Unless you instruct us otherwise*. In Example b the modifier *in the rear* has a word to modify, *engine*, but because of its placement, *in the rear* seems to modify *horizontally opposed*. The result is confusion.

9a.   The implied subject of an introductory modifier must be the same as the grammatical subject of the clause that follows.

Example: *When standing in front of the door, the glass takes on a reflective quality.*

Correction: *When someone stands in front of the door, the glass takes on a reflective quality.*

Alternate correction: *Seen from the front, the glass casts a reflection.*

Explanation: The **participial modifier,** *standing,* has no **referent** to modify. This situation occurs so often that some manuals call such introductory modifiers "dangling participles." **Participle** or not, if the phrase at the beginning has an implied subject, it must be the same as the grammatical subject of the clause that follows. In the first correction, the subject of *stand* is not implied but stated. This clause is grammatically correct. The second correction uses the participial modifier *seen.* What is seen is the glass; therefore the sentence is correct.

The dangling modifier need not necessarily be a participle. In the following example, the introductory phrase contains no participle, in fact no modifier at all. But the phrase as a whole is an adverbial modifier, and the key word, *interaction,* has an implied subject.

> *Through informal interaction with colleagues, ideas may be exchanged regarding procedures, policies, courses, or programs.*

The best correction of this sentence puts the **main clause** in the active form, improving two elements of the sentence at once:

> *Through informal interaction, colleagues may exchange ideas regarding procedures, policies, courses, or programs.*

The crucial correction, however, is that the implied subject of *interaction* must be the same as the grammatical subject of the clause that follows.

9b.   Place modifiers carefully to avoid confusion.

Example: *You don't see a building like this with so much architectural detail too often for industrial use.*

Correction: *You don't often see an industrial building with so much architectural detail.*

Explanation: This sentence has two misplaced modifying phrases: *too often* and *for industrial use*. As the phrases are moved to the right places, it becomes apparent that both phrases can be shortened to streamline the sentence at the same time.

Creating a special problem are those modifiers at the end of a sentence, remote from the words they modify. They seem tacked on.

Example: *In an attempt to retrieve rhetoric from the ridicule of Plato and his followers, Hermagoras adapted the theory of stasis, which had been used by Aristotle in both his scientific studies and his* Rhetoric, *to the study of rhetoric.*

Correction: *To retrieve rhetoric from the ridicule of Plato and his followers, Hermagoras adapted to rhetoric the theory of stasis, which Aristotle had used in both his scientific studies and his* Rhetoric.

Explanation: As a writer begins to improve the sample sentence, several improvements suggest themselves. *In an attempt to retrieve* can be shortened. The passive *which had been used by Aristotle* sounds better in the active form, *which Aristotle had used*. The important change, however, is placing *to the study of rhetoric* in shortened form, beside the verb it modifies.

10.   Choose the proper pronoun.

Personal pronouns and relative pronouns present different kinds of problems arising from their different grammatical functions. In selecting the right personal pronoun, the issue is **case**, whether the pronoun is in the subject or the object form.

> Example: *Who we select for the assignment will depend on who is in the office that day.*

The proper form for the first word in the sentence is the object form, *whom*. The second use of *who* is correct.

In selecting relative pronouns the writer must decide whether to use *which, that,* or *who*.

> Example: *The rules of the company prevent us from considering an applicant which is related to a company officer.*

The proper pronoun here is *who* because the applicant is clearly a person, not a thing.

10a.   Use the object form if the pronoun is object of a verb or object of a preposition.

> Example: *The computer selected him as the ideal partner for Denise.*

This sentence needs no correction. Any native speaker would use the **object form** *him* after *selected*. When there are multiple objects of a verb, however, the choice of forms is not so easy.

> Example: *The team members have selected Osborn and I to direct the investigation.*

> Correction: *The team members have selected Osborn and me to direct the investigation.*

Explanation: This situation causes trouble because two deeply ingrained rules conflict. We are taught early to correct *Me and Laura went to the movies* to *Laura and I went to the movies.* For pairs of persons we name the other person first and refer to ourselves as I. And yet we also know to use the object form of pronouns for objects of verbs or objects of **prepositions**. Because the two rules conflict in the example above, we may make the wrong choice. The way to test which pronoun fits is to put the pronouns in separate sentences: *The team members have selected Osborn* and *The team members have selected me.*

Who presents a special problem. Because it may introduce a question, *who* often appears at the beginning of a sentence.

Example: *Who will direct this operation?*

Example: *Who will the company send to Detroit?*

The first of these sentences presents no problem; *who* is the proper form. The second sentence introduces another conflict of internalized rules: (1) use *who* at the beginning of a sentence, and (2) use *whom* for the object of a verb. This dilemma has no correct solution. For informal communications it is probably better to use *who*, for more formal communications, *whom*.

The rules for *whoever* and *whomever* are the same as those for *who* and *whom*. Because *whomever* occurs seldom in speech, it may sound stuffy, foreign to the ear, whether it is correct or incorrect.

Example a: *I will send the letter to whomever you have nominated.*

Example b: *We can measure what is happening in our programs and report the results to whomever is interested.*

Correction a: *None. The sentence is correct.*

Correction b: *We can measure what is happening in our programs and report the results to whoever is interested.*

Explanation: In example b, the pronoun is the subject of an imbedded clause, *whoever is interested.* The **nominative** or subject form is correct. Because *whomever* follows immediately after *to*, the writer has been tricked into treating the pronoun as object of the preposition. An additional example, made up for the occasion, will illustrate the best way to approach sentences of this sort.

Give the prize to whoever you think will win.

The pronoun is between the preposition *to* and the subject-verb combination *you think.* There are two reasons, therefore, to suspect the correct form is *whomever.* But *whoever* is the subject of a clause that is embedded twice:

Give the prize to [you think (___ will win)].

10b.   Use *that* or *which* with inanimate referents, *who* or *whom* with human referents.

Example: *The award went to a promising new writer that happens to be a member of this department.*

Correction: *The award went to a promising new writer who happens to be a member of this department.*

Explanation: The writer of this sentence may have thought *that* refers to an abstract concept, *a promising new writer*, and therefore should have the form for inanimate **referents**. It should be clear, however, that writers, as used in this context, are human and that members of the department are human as well. Another reason for choosing *that* is to fit the rule about restrictive clauses, mentioned below. In modern usage, however, choosing *who* for persons takes precedence over choosing *that* for restrictive modifiers.

Most professional writers violate this rule if observing it would result in a convoluted sentence.

Example: *It is a complex organization whose regulations are frustrating to ordinary investors.*

To follow the rule about inanimate referents, the writer would have to say,

> *It is a complex organization the regulations of which are frustrating to ordinary investors.*

Because *which* has no possessive form, the writer must choose between violating the rule about inanimate referents and constructing an awkward sentence.

An additional rule about *that* and *which* requires *that* in restrictive clauses, *which* in nonrestrictive clauses:

Example a: *Every department has a writing intensive course that all of its majors must take.*

Example b: *Your department should use the new Canon copier, which is located in room 107.*

Explanation: The distinction between restrictive and nonrestrictive modifiers will be treated again in the chapter on punctuation. Simply put, restrictive clauses provide essential, identifying information about the nouns they modify. Nonrestrictive clauses provide parenthetical, non-identifying information. A rule of thumb is, if the clause is nonrestrictive, you will probably hear a slight pause and reflect that pause by inserting a comma. The proper pronoun in that case is *which.* You should be aware, however, that the rule governing *that* and *which* is for formal occasions and is frequently ignored by successful professional writers. For most occasions, certainly for informal writing, choosing the wrong pronoun will not ruin your prose.

10c. Make sure the referent (antecedent) of a pronoun is clear.

Example: *Long after the hostilities were ended, the citizens distrusted foreign visitors because they were unfamiliar with the terms of the treaty.*

Correction: *Long after the hostilities were ended, the citizens distrusted foreign visitors because the visitors were unfamiliar with the terms of the treaty.*

Explanation: In the example sentence, *they* is ambiguous. To correct the sentence, I have guessed the **antecedent** of *they* is visitors, not *citizens*. By repeating *the visitors* I have made the sentence slightly clumsy. Better clumsy than confusing.

Example: *The office is now supplied with a laser printer which puts desk-top publishing well within our reach.*

Correction: *The office is now supplied with a laser printer that puts desk-top publishing within our reach.*

Alternate correction: *The office is now supplied with a laser printer, which puts desk-top publishing within our reach.*

Second alternate correction: *The office is now supplied with a laser printer; the addition puts desk-top publishing within our reach.*

Explanation: The example is ambiguous. We don't know whether *which* refers to *laser printer* or whether it sums up the whole main clause. The first correction makes the clause restrictive by using *that* to modify *printer*. The alternate correction suggests that *which* in the original sentence refers to the whole main clause. The comma after *printer* indicates the *which* clause is nonrestrictive and probably not compatible with *a laser printer.* To eliminate confusion, in the second alternate correction I have replaced *which* with an unambiguous noun phrase.

10d.   Never use the reflexive form of a pronoun for the subject of a sentence.

The intrusion of a **reflexive pronoun** is never a problem when the pronoun is the sole grammatical subject. No native speaker of English would say, *Myself went to the plant show at the Botanical Garden.* We might, however, be tempted to write, *My two neighbors and myself went to the plant show at the Botanical Garden.* We are especially tempted to use the reflexive form when the pronoun is in an appositive phrase renaming the grammatical subject:

> *The three men in this class—Father Rankin, Dr. McClary, and myself—are uncomfortable with the selection of texts.*

The proper form of the pronoun is nominative case, the subject form:

> *The three men in this class—Father Rankin, Dr. McClary, and I—are uncomfortable with the selection of texts.*

The reflexive form should be reserved for reflexive uses:

> *Because I was careless, I injured myself using the weed-eater.*

or:

> *I addressed the letter to myself so that I would know when it arrived.*

The rule about reserving the reflexive form for reflexive uses applies to pronouns in the object position as well as those in the subject position. We should not say,

The property was released to my sister and myself after the legal fees were paid.

The sentence should read, instead:

The property was released to my sister and me after the legal fees were paid.

11. Avoid separating subject and verb.

A minor guideline with many exceptions, this rule can be illustrated by sample sentences.

Example: *I, with the assistance of some students, developed a teaching unit on coping with divorce.*

Correction: *With the assistance of some students I developed a teaching unit on coping with divorce.*

Example: Gone with the Wind, *when it was published, was an immediate best seller.*

Correction: *When it was published,* Gone with the Wind *was an immediate best seller.*

Explanation: Notice that changing the order of these sentences does not change their meaning or their force. Their directness, therefore, is improved by putting the subject and verb together.

Often it will seem right to separate subject and verb:

Example: *Our new car, damaged in the garage fire, is worthless.*

To change this sentence—*Damaged in the garage fire, our new car is worthless*—would remove the punch achieved by placing the subject at the beginning.

The key to distinguishing between these two situations is whether the intervening modifier is an **adjectival** element, modifying the subject, or an **adverbial** element, modifying the verb. Notice what happens in the sentence about *Gone with the Wind* if we make the modifier an adjective phrase:

> Example: Gone with the Wind, *Mitchell's only novel, was an immediate best seller.*

Here the modifier is not felt as an interruption. The general wisdom is, if an adverbial **clause** or **phrase** comes between the subject and the verb, move it to the beginning of the sentence.

12.   Keep coordinate elements in parallel form.

The **syntax** of a sentence reflects how its parts fit together. A writer can help the reader see how words or phrases are related by keeping parallel elements in similar form. Attention to **parallel structure** provides a check on the thinking behind the words.

> Example: *I put a toothpick in my mouth and suck and gnaw at it until either I feel better or until there is nothing left but splinters.*

> Correction: *I put a toothpick in my mouth and suck and gnaw at it either until I feel better or until there is nothing left but splinters.*

> Alternate correction: *I put a toothpick in my mouth and suck and gnaw at it until either I feel better or I have nothing left to chew.*

Explanation: In any sentence with *either . . . or*, what follows *either* must have the same grammatical structure as what follows *or*. In the first correction *either* is placed before *until* so that the clauses following *either* and *or* both begin with *until*. In the alternate correction the second *until* is removed. The second **subordinate clause** has been modified to match the structure of the first, *I* followed by a verb. The alternate correction is not grammatically necessary, but it makes the sentence balance better.

Example: *In our government many women have careers in the House of Representatives, the Senate, the Presidential Cabinet, or on the Supreme Court.*

Correction: *In our government many women have careers in the House of Representatives, in the Senate, in the Presidential Cabinet, or on the Supreme Court.*

Alternate correction: *In our government many women have careers in the House of Representatives, the Senate, or the Presidential Cabinet, or on the Supreme Court.*

Explanation: The example contains four items, presumably in a series. The series could consist of objects of the preposition *in*, but the Supreme Court throws the series off. By convention judges serve *on* the Supreme Court. In the first correction, the structure is changed to a series of prepositional phrases, each with its own preposition. In the second correction, the preposition *in* is treated as having three objects, with *or* separating the second and third, and *on the Supreme Court* is handled as a separate construction, not part of the series.

To provide one more illustration of faulty parallel structure, I return to the writer with the toothpick:

I guess I look at my toothpick as a smoker would a cigarette or how a baby would its thumb.

The simplest way to improve this sentence is to use a connecting phrase that will sound natural with both clauses:

I guess I look at my toothpick the way a smoker would a cigarette or a baby would its thumb.

13.   Avoid the most damaging spelling errors.

This guide to style and mechanics makes no systematic effort to deal with spelling. The writer's most useful resources for spelling are a dictionary and a computer's spelling checker. If you are not sure how to spell *prerogative* or *remuneration*, you must look up the word. Remember, some errors in spelling will not be caught by the spelling checker because alternate spellings are also valid words. Often such words are so familiar that we don't think to look them up. Misspelling these words may result from simple carelessness, or it may result from honest confusion.

13a.   Be alert to the difference between plural and possessive.

The spelling rules governing plurals and **possessives** are simple to explain and easy to follow. In general, to make nouns plural, we add –s or –es. The possessive is formed by adding an apostrophe, either before or after the s, depending on whether the noun is singular or plural. When writers use the wrong form, it is usually because their attention has wandered.

Example: *Our books jackets are designed by commercial artists.*

Correction: *Our books' jackets are designed by commercial artists.*

Alternate correction: *The jackets of our books are designed by commercial artists.*

Explanation: The sound of *books' jackets* in the first corrected sentence may bother a reader because both nouns end in s. The repetition of the final consonants, one indicating possessive, the other plural, is avoided in the alter-

nate correction. A third correction, treating *book* as a
noun adjunct and eliminating the *s* altogether, is also
possible:

> *Our book jackets are designed by a commercial artist.*

13b.   Watch out for troublesome pairs: its/it's, their/there, to/too.

At issue here are pairs of words, often **homonyms**, that
a spelling checker will not catch because both are legitimate words, correctly spelled. A list of troublesome pairs
will illustrate.

its/it's	*their/there/they're*
to/two/too	*here/hear*
your/you're	*whose/who's*

Of the careless substitutions, the most damaging is
between *its* and *it's*. The two forms are confusing because
the rules for plural and possessive seem to switch. *Its*, without an apostrophe, is the possessive form. The rules have
not really changed; personal pronouns never form their
possessives with an apostrophe. The apostrophe in *it's*
signifies a contraction of *it is*. But we may forget, momen-
tarily, that *it* is a personal pronoun. The reason the error is
so damaging is that the rule is so simple. Almost no reader
tolerates this error as simple carelessness. You can hear the
editor, the teacher, the supervisor: "This clown doesn't know
the difference between a possessive and a contraction!"

Many adult writers confuse *then* and *than*. They know
the difference; they carelessly substitute one for another.

14.   Pay attention to conspicuous comma errors.

The guidelines here will be covered again in the chapter
on punctuation, but they deserve special attention as editing guidelines. Many readers will not regard mishandling

of a compound sentence as a simple punctuation error. They will treat it as a sentence error, one of the most serious editing gaffes. Some of these guidelines are not covered in punctuation manuals except by omission. The writers of punctuation manuals often forget to tell us where not to put commas.

14a.   If two or more independent clauses are joined together, they should be linked with a comma and a conjunction or with a semicolon.

Understanding this guideline depends on knowing that clauses are called **independent** if they can be treated as separate sentences, each with its own capital letter at the beginning and period at the end. **Dependent clauses** cannot stand alone. *It rained all afternoon* is an independent clause and could be a sentence. But in *Because it rained all afternoon, we never left the house*, the first clause is dependent.

Consider two short sentences:

a: *Understanding the guidelines in this book is easy.*
b: *Putting the guidelines to work will take practice.*

We could combine them using a comma and **conjunction**:

> *Understanding the guidelines in this book is easy, but putting them to work will take practice.*

We could as easily link them with a semicolon:

> *Understanding the guidelines in this book is easy; putting them to work will take practice.*

We must have some connecting punctuation because both are independent clauses. If we subordinate one clause by adding a **subordinating conjunction**, the rules change. When the subordinate clause comes first, it is set off by a comma:

> *Although understanding the guidelines in this book is easy, putting them to work will take practice.*

We normally do not set off a subordinate clause when it follows the main clause:

> *Putting the guidelines to work will take practice even though they are easy to learn.*

We will return to introductory clauses in 14d.

14b. When two clauses are joined to form a compound sentence, the comma separating them goes in front of the conjunction.

Example: *Developing leadership is the mission of this university so, it is fitting that community leaders gather here to contemplate our future.*

Correction: *Developing leadership is the mission of this university, so it is fitting that community leaders gather here to contemplate our future.*

Alternate correction: *Developing leadership is the mission of this university; it is fitting, therefore, that community leaders gather here to contemplate our future.*

Explanation: The writer of the example sentence may have been told to put a comma wherever she or he felt a pause was appropriate. Thinking of an oral delivery, the writer felt it was natural to pause for effect after the conjunction *so*. But the rules for punctuating a **compound sentence** are tied to the grammar of the clauses, not to the sound.

14c. Avoid separating subject and verb by a comma.

Example a: *Every student on this list from the Registrar, made at least a C in freshman composition.*

Example b: *A writer who takes such a reading level seriously and without full understanding, risks obscuring the prose to achieve a different mark.*

Correction a: *Every student on this list from the Registrar made at least a C in freshman composition.*

Correction b: *A writer who takes such a reading level seriously and without full understanding risks obscuring the prose to achieve a different mark.*

Explanation: The cause of the error, when it occurs, is the mistaken impulse to put a comma wherever a reader might normally pause or take a breath. But remember the principle mentioned in 14b: the rules for punctuating a compound sentence are tied to the grammar of the clauses, not to the sound. The same is true of sentences that seem long enough to be compound sentences but are not.

Example b of this guideline was taken from an early draft of this manuscript. I put the comma in because I was listening to the sentence as I wrote, not paying attention to the grammatical structure. The correction I actually made was not to remove the comma after *understanding*. Instead, I added a comma after *seriously*, treating *and without full understanding* as a parenthetical addition.

Alternate correction b: *A writer who takes such a reading level seriously, and without full understanding, risks obscuring the prose to achieve a different mark.*

14d. Use a comma after an introductory clause or sentence modifier.

Understanding this guideline requires mastering two important distinctions. The first is between **clauses** and

phrases; introductory clauses require a comma, short adverbial phrases do not. A clause is a group of words containing both a subject and a **finite verb**; a phrase is a group of words lacking either a subject or a finite verb or both.

> Example a (introductory clause): *When the inventory is complete the clerk should check the appropriate box on the form.*
>
> Correction: *When the inventory is complete, the clerk should check the appropriate box on the form.*
>
> Example b (introductory phase): *After the third game the coach made some personnel adjustments, and the team's record improved.*
>
> Correction: *None. The punctuation is correct.*

Explanation: The introductory syntactic unit in example a is a clause, including a subject, *the inventory*, and a **predicating verb** (or finite verb), *is complete*. An introductory clause requires a comma. The introductory unit in example b is a prepositional phrase, without a subject and a finite verb.

The rule governing introductory phrases relies on the discretion of the writer. If the phrase is short, not more than five or six words, no comma is required. If the phrase is long or might be confusing, a comma is needed:

> *After the shift to Daylight Saving Time in the spring, our work schedule is adjusted to allow more flexible hours.*

The second distinction is between true adverbial modifiers and **sentence modifiers** such as *nevertheless, on the other hand, however.* Consider the following sentences:

> a. *Gradually the blossom turned to face the sun.*
>
> b. *Frankly, the tone of this letter is insincere.*

In sentence a, *gradually* is a true adverb, modifying the verb *turned.* The sentence requires no comma. In sentence b, *frankly* does not modify the verb; it modifies the whole sentence and indicates something about the manner in which the sentence is delivered or intended. Convention holds that introductory sentence modifiers are set off by commas.

This rule explains why we normally set off *nevertheless* and *however* at the beginning of a clause and do not set off simple conjunctions such as *but* or doubled conjunctions such as *and yet*. But the rule is not automatic and may be difficult to apply. We'll return to this construction in the chapter on punctuation.

EXERCISES

The exercises in this section match the editing guidelines in Chapter Two. For these editing problems, as for the composing exercises following Chapter One, no single correct solution can be offered. Careful attention to the guidelines, however, should help you discover how the sentences can be improved.

8.   Use singular verbs with single subjects, plural verbs with plural subjects.

Directions: Select the proper form of the verb, where a choice is indicated, and make any other changes needed to correct subject-verb agreement in the following sentences.

1. Each of the books we have chosen have soft covers.

2. The library's collection of government documents are housed in the library annex.

3. Neither of these arrangements present a satisfactory solution to our traffic problem.

4. There's two good reasons for closing the office on Saturdays.

5. Every person in the office or all of them together have a chance to influence the choice of a new chief executive.

6. Hightower is one of the candidates who has endorsed the workers' compensation bill.

7. The conductor of the orchestra, along with six other musicians, (leaves/leave) for Germany next month.

8. All of the local union members and their national representative has signed the letter of complaint.

9. None of the neighborhood residents were present at the City Council meeting.

10. A number of our newest acquisitions has already been checked out by students.

11. Along with a new baby comes a lot of choices.

12. The faculty are divided on whether to support the proposed curriculum revision.

9. Avoid dangling and misplaced modifiers.

Directions: Rearrange or revise the following sentences to eliminate error or confusion.

1. Before entering college, my mother often told me college would be the best years of my life.

2. As an individual investing your own hard earned dollars, we think you'll be interested in what our company has to offer.

3. While difficult to quantify, it seems obvious that our image as a major university would be enhanced by an engineering program of high quality.

4. [From a TV commercial] Come and see Rick Waters. There are no attorney's fees unless successful.

5. By thumbing the "great authors" day and night, absorbing their thoughts, relishing their words, their expertise and ideals will become the student's.

6. We are not an elitist university. We seek to attract talented students who are capable of taking on society's important challenges, however.

7. We'll have to do what counts most first and accept that we must put off what doesn't touch our lives directly until later.

8. By putting the rebellion in its historical setting and examining the economic conditions of the time, it becomes clear that more was at stake than personal freedom or individual rights.

9. Through careful negotiations with management, some improvement of the office conditions under which we work may be achieved.

10. Erosion of the soil around the foundation may create conditions that cause walls to crack slowly.

11. The supplemental pages include procedures for installing the new control devices which may be different from the ones you are using.

12. Carrying a stack of plates, balanced precariously, the waiter turned the corner on one foot.

13. The crowd greeted the candidate as she entered the hall, chanting, "Four more years!"

10. Choose the proper pronoun.

Direction: In the following sentences correct the pronouns that are incorrect or likely to cause confusion.

1. When I went home to visit, I felt like a person that had been transformed without knowing it.

2. Stephen Jobs applied Quantitative Management

Theory to Apple Computer, Inc. This was important to apply, especially in the computer industry, because it is dynamic and complex.

3. With the advent of the printing press, readers had a greater sense of contact with writers which heightened their interest.

4. Disembarking onto the beautiful white sand of Gardner Bay, a group of seven travelers and myself, with our naturalist guide, made our way along the beach.

5. Who do you expect to finish the race first?

6. The group of senators which had opposed this bill found themselves embarrassed by its defeat.

7. The committee appointed to work on employee benefits spent their time handling individual grievances.

8. You can pick whoever you like. Any of our trainees can do the work.

9. Once you have enrolled with our company, you will be assigned a representative that will make an appointment to discuss the benefits.

10. Mr. Mendez was able to talk with the senator because he happened to come through the door at just the right moment.

11. The following passage from a manual on field education for social work needs tightening in several ways. A conspicuous weakness is in the use of pronouns: *such* and two uses of *it*. Revise the passage to clarify meaning and tighten the prose.

For students field learning has always received high marks and been viewed as a key element in their social work education. As such, field education is one of the essential elements in each student's learning experience. Because it occupies such an important place, field education is the focus for many of the issues which confront the relationship between social work education and social work practice. The relationship of the two systems is essential for field learning which is educationally directed. Because of its importance, the field is a charged area for both practice and education.

11.   Avoid separating subject and verb.

Directions: Rewrite the following sentences to keep subject and verb together if possible. You may want to leave some sentences alone.

1. My sister, when she discovered the fire ants, tried to call off the picnic.

2. The new publishing company, because it produces mainly manuals and catalogues, will not attract many literary figures.

3. Evelyn, seeing the auditorium packed with parents and friends, panicked and forgot her speech.

4. The excited children, clapping and cheering, burst through the schoolroom door.

5. "The Great Emancipator," which is the name some historians gave to Abraham Lincoln, was assassinated during his second term of office.

6. Students, who often may be oppressed by deadlines, are tempted to seek out publishing companies that produce term papers.

7. Rodney Buckford, the new shortstop, has been an important addition to our team.

8. Rodney Buckford, in the season opener, hit a homerun.

12.   Keep coordinate elements in parallel form.

Directions: Rewrite the following sentences so as to help the reader by having coordinate elements in parallel form.

1. Women had to limit what they said, did, or write in order to succeed.

2. Early in the epidemic, what attitude to take towards AIDS patients and what language chosen to describe them became matters of debate.

3. Such rapid development in knowledge serves as an example of the ability of "good research" to target and then work quickly and efficiently to solve tragic human problems.

4. A few preliminary cautions will help to avoid trouble: (1) the optimum temperature for the CRT terminal is between 65 and 75 degrees; (2) don't allow the terminal to be operated excessively; (3) the terminal is not mobile and should not be moved; (4) due to the sensitivity of the machine, no smoking is allowed near the terminal.

5. As the examination of the major rhetoricians progresses, we will consider historical setting, the educational reforms undertaken by each man, the prevailing political and social climate, and we shall ask how and why cultural literacy and rhetoric were important in each instance.

6. Of course there are men upon whom the burdens of divorce and the sacrifices required to raise children have fallen or been taken on with equal weight.

7. The stasis theory gave those unschooled in dialectic a starting point from which to begin a successful dialogue either with a person or a text.

8. Cultivating audience awareness allowed Luther and his contemporaries to prove not only the inconsistencies in the claims made by the Church, but to unite common folk in a way previously unknown.

9. Printing allowed easier circulation of ideas, adaptation of those ideas to a new historical context, and opened the door to new study methods as students began to own their own copies of important texts.

10. A formal organization of any kind has both a structure and a set of procedures, both formal and informal, which deal with the decision making process, getting the work done, informing people about what is happening, establishment of accountability, and affirming rules or guidelines for interaction between persons.

13.   Avoid the most damaging spelling errors.

Directions: Each of the following sentences requires a choice between two words that sound alike.

1. When the bell sounds, (its/it's) time to close the door.

2. This engine seems to have (its/it's) own personality.

3. The touring players found (there/their) way to the center of town.

4. If (there/their) are any new books in, you'll find them in a box by the door.

5. We are all (to/too) tired to try again.

6. The child swam (to/too) the raft and back.

7. Mr. Elroy, (to/too), will attend the service.

8. I want to know (whose/who's) baseball glove is on the back porch.

9. Please let the office know (whose/who's) going to greet the new employees.

10. You'll have to answer (your/you're) own phone.

11. If (your/you're) ready to begin, turn to page three in (your/you're) test booklet.

12. We like to (here/hear) success stories.

13. (Here/Hear) now, what are you doing with that book?

14.   Pay attention to conspicuous comma errors.

Directions: Correct the punctuation in the following sentences. You may need to make other changes.

1. The average man's definition of himself does not include the wants of women, therefore, he concludes that he does not understand women.

2. I will be out of my office next week so you will not be able to come for a conference.

3. Piaget's studies with children brought him recognition as a child psychologist, he is the world's acknowledged expert in the area of cognitive development.

4. Literature is a social institution, Plato in effect affirmed, as such it must be judged by social standards.

5. Some feelings are kindled only to smoulder away and leave dead ashes, others tend to kindle on and on, awakening thought, rousing to vigorous action.

Each of the following groups of clauses can be grouped together in one or two sentences. Combine them and provide appropriate punctuation.

6. Persuasion, according to the sophists, fails to consider the interests of the hearer.

Frequently it even assails them.

In fact the sophistic precepts imply the hearer's part in discourse is spoiled.

7. Your resume should make you sound like an achiever.

Forget your negative aspects.

Stress your positive attributes.

8. The participants are to remain anonymous.

They should use only their assigned numbers on the form.

They should not sign the form.

9. My own writing takes me by surprise.

I don't know what I will say until I say it.

I don't know what I have said until I hear it.

10. In my opinion this is not merely a good book.

    It is a great book.

    It cannot fail to make its mark.

Directions: Punctuate the following sentences. You may discover that deciding on the placement of commas depends on your understanding of a sentence.

11. Honestly I can't understand your position on mandatory insurance.

12. I can't honestly support your position on mandatory insurance.

13. A ballplayer preoccupied with her batting average risks sacrificing the team's success for her own glory.

14. The desire to solve all problems and to answer all questions was more than a vague dream of these early scientists.

15. After a quick survey of the list of authors in the third chapter she was able to locate the quotation.

16. Before examining these samples I want to verify the location of the accident.

17. To be frank your explanation of the process is difficult to follow.

18. Again I apologize for my delay in getting this tape to you.

19. Every one of the students on this chart has met the composition requirements of our college.

20. Hopefully every person we have asked to participate will return the data card before the closing date.

Chapter Three

Punctuation

SUMMARY ESSAY

Most writers get through most writing assignments with a small collection of punctuation tools and a narrow range of strategies. Periods and commas may be all we ever use. For the writing we do every day—letters to friends, memos to fellow office workers, and simple reports—periods and commas are probably enough.

Punctuating the ends of sentences is easy. We can choose from period, question mark, and exclamation point. Each mark has a specific purpose, and we make the choice as we go along, in the composing stage. A question is a question, is it not? We recognize the question as we write it. And when we want to make a point emphatic, most of us know how to use an exclamation point. Of course! For all other sentences the period is the correct terminal punctuation.

Distributing commas is more tricky. Commas must be arranged within the sentences. They reflect either the grammatical structure of a sentence or, perhaps, the breathing pauses or the way we modulate our voices as we read each sentence. Rules govern the placement of commas, we are led to believe, but no one seems to know the rules. Putting in commas, therefore, is a guessing game we play in the revision and editing stages, after the sentences are written.

The approach in this guide will be to start simple, getting down terminal punctuation and the most fundamental uses of commas—the rules, such as they are. Handling standard punctuation is crucial. If you make a mistake in the punctuation of independent clauses, you will draw fire from critics. If you mismanage the punctuation of a tricky series, you may confuse your readers. If you can master the essentials, however, you should be able to process prose that does not call attention to itself. The paradox is that punctuation errors jump off the page to dance in front of watchful critics, yet no one gets credit for punctuating correctly. The goal of a writer is to handle routine punctuation so deftly that no one will ever notice.

After presenting the essential rules and addressing some of the trouble spots, I'll move on to more interesting and sophisticated uses of punctuation. For a mature writer punctuation can be a valuable resource. Punctuation can open possibilities in the composition of sentences, possibilities we might otherwise overlook. Moreover, the adroit handling of semicolons, colons, and dashes can make writing stylish, can give it a flair your more discriminating readers will appreciate.

Some of the material in this chapter has already been covered in Chapter Two. The argument for having a self-contained chapter on punctuation is strong enough to risk repetition.

GUIDELINES

Essentials

15. Punctuate the end of a sentence with a period, a question mark, or an exclamation point.

The period [.] is the standard mark of punctuation for most sentences. If you don't know what a **declarative sentence** is, you can rely on knowing that if there is no reason to use a question mark or an exclamation point, the normal terminal punctuation is a period.

The question mark [?] has a limited and specific use. If the sentence is a question, the correct terminal punctuation is a question mark.

Example: *Have you found the book you were looking for?*

Example: *How shall we approach this difficult assignment?*

The situation that most often causes indecision is a question embedded in a declarative sentence. Consider the following sentences:

a. *Mr. Kelsey wants to know if we are going to the football game.*
b. *Mr. Kelsey has asked, are we going to the football game?*
c. *Are we going to the football game, Mr. Kelsey wonders.*

In example a, the question is indirect and the sentence is declarative. The important consideration in b and c is whether the sentence ends as a question or as a statement. Example b, ending in a question, is punctuated as a question; example c is treated as a statement. The intention of the writer is also important. If the writer wanted to shift the focus to who asked the question, example b could end with a period. The writer has a choice.

Another kind of sentence that may present a difficult decision is a sentence that has the form of a question but has the rhetorical force of a statement or an exclamation.

Example: *How could my neighbor do such a thing.*

This sentence, in question form, could easily be punctuated as a question:

How could my neighbor do such a thing?

But the force of the sentence is not so much to inquire as to make a declarative statement. If the writer chose, the sentence might just as easily end in an exclamation point:

How could my neighbor do such a thing!

The choice of terminal punctuation, here as in the sentences with indirect questions, depends on the intention of the writer more than on the form of the sentence.

The exclamation point [!] is for emphatic commands or expressions of surprise.

Example: *Don't open that door!*

Example: *Gracious! I never saw such a mess.*

The important rule governing exclamation points is use them sparingly. Good modern prose is seldom sprinkled with exclamation points. If your goal is to make your prose strong and emphatic, the challenge is to achieve strength and emphasis by constructing good sentences. Adding exclamation points will almost surely reduce the force of your prose, not increase it, because the exclamation points will draw attention to themselves.

Another important rule about exclamation points: never use more than one exclamation point at the end of a sentence. Only bad advertising copy would punctuate sentences this way:

SALE!!! Come in early! Beat the crowd!!!

Good advertising copy would be more sophisticated.

The most important consideration in placing terminal punctuation, and often the most ticklish, is where each sentence ends. If we write as we speak, we will often string together clauses and phrases that make up sentences of a fairly sophisticated variety, but often without being conscious of when one sentence ends and the next begins. Consider the following passage:

This book is like a bush; it grows from a single root, many branches, many leaves and twigs, but all the

> *same plant. Many resemblances, as one branch and its*
> *leaves look like another, except when you look closely.*
> *But there the whole thing is: structure and foliage. And*
> *there is a plan, which was gradually disclosed to me as*
> *I wrote.*   [Centering, p. 5]

Notice that the punctuation can be altered without making the passage incoherent or obviously wrong. The first semicolon could be a period. But if there were a period following *a single root*, the remaining phrases, *many branches, many leaves and twigs, but all the same plant*, would be stranded as an incomplete fragment. The sentence, *Many resemblances, as one branch and its leaves look like another, except when you look closely*, is in fact a grammatical fragment. The writer has forced us to supply a verb for the sentence: *[It has] Many resemblances. . . .* Although this punctuation and this omission constitute a conscious stylistic maneuver, appropriate for the book in which it appears, they would not be acceptable in a formal report.

A less artistic example, taken from a newspaper, may bring the point closer to home:

> *The package may be smaller, but it's still the same*
> *Max Marlin Fitzwater. Bald and ruddy-faced, with a*
> *self-deprecating humor that never falters—even under*
> *the enormity of international crises, White House in-*
> *fighting and the constant recognition that he could*
> *start a war with a slip of the tongue.*
>   [Fort Worth Star-Telegram, Nov. 19, 1989]

Although it is punctuated as two sentences, this passage is really a single sentence. The second part, beginning *Bald and ruddy-faced*, is an adjective phrase modifying *Fitzwater*. The editor of the newspaper apparently felt that a paragraph of a single sentence would look wrong.

The rules to remember in checking for sentence errors are two:

1. *Every sentence must have a subject and a finite verb.*
2. *To link two independent clauses requires more than a comma.*

Example: *The point being, you have to have a membership card to shop at this economy outlet.*

Correction: *The point is, you have to have a membership card to shop at this economy outlet.*

In the example, *being* is not a finite verb. To make the sentence complete, *being* must be replaced by *is*.

Example: *Alfred arrived for the exam on time, the others were at least thirty minutes late.*

Correction: *Alfred arrived for the exam on time, but the others were at least thirty minutes late.*

Alternate correction: *Alfred arrived for the exam on time; the others were at least thirty minutes late.*

In the example, two independent clauses have been linked by a comma. To make the sentence correct, either add a conjunction or use a semicolon to link the sentences. We'll return to linking clauses in a compound sentence at least twice more before we are through.

16.   Follow the rules governing commas.

Commas are used for three purposes: linking, as between clauses in a sentence; separating, as between items in a series; and enclosing, as in setting off parenthetical information. A summary of the rules for commas is presented at the end of this section.

16a. Use commas to link.

We have just been through the linking of clauses in a compound sentence. The rule given above was, "To link two independent clauses requires more than a comma." The implication is, most situations require a comma and a conjunction. The comma must precede the conjunction.

> Example: *The law requires a prosecutor to prove a defendant's guilt and only solid evidence and reasoned argument can prove anything.*

> Correction: *The law requires a prosecutor to prove a defendant's guilt, and only solid evidence and reasoned argument can prove anything.*

The rule is simple. The tricky part is recognizing where one independent clause ends and another begins.

> Example: *A good lawyer knows the difference between letting the evide nce make the client's case and hanging the client out on a limb.*

Although this is a fairly long sentence, it contains only one independent clause. No commas are needed.

> Example: *My father hung up his hat when he came through the door.*

Because the second part of the sentence is a dependent clause, not an independent clause, no comma separates the clauses. A dependent clause (also called a subordinate clause) is normally set off with a comma when it precedes the main clause, but not set off with a comma when it follows the main clause.

A simple way to recognize main clauses making up compound sentences is to learn a short list of **coordinating conjunctions**:

<u>COORDINATING CONJUNCTIONS</u>

and	*yet*
but	*so*
or	*for*
nor	

These coordinating conjunctions link main clauses. All the other normal conjunctions—*when, after, because, until,* and the like—are subordinating conjunctions and introduce subordinate clauses.

An optional exception to the rule about putting a comma before the conjunction in a compound sentence allows a writer to omit the comma if the two clauses are fairly short and closely related, especially if the two clauses have the same subject.

Example: *The porter found the door open and he walked in.*

Example: *We know you are tired and we want you to rest.*

Both of these sentences are short, and in each the subject is the same in both clauses. It would be possible in each of these sentences to use a comma only and omit the conjunction.

Example: *The porter found the door open, he walked in.*

Example: *We know you are tired, we want you to rest.*

This situation is delicate and rare. For most sentences it is best to observe the general rule: between two independent clauses use a comma and a conjunction.

16b.   Use commas to separate.

The distinction between coordinating conjunctions and subordinating conjunctions is useful for the most troublesome of separating commas, the comma that sets off an introductory clause. The general rule is this: if a group of introductory words is a clause, set if off with a comma; if the group of words is a phrase used as a simple adverb, do not.

> Example a: *If the other person does not answer, hang up the phone.*

> Example b: *After the fourth ring hang up.*

The first word in example a is a subordinating conjunction. The group of words it introduces, *if the other person does not answer*, is a clause containing a subject, *person*, and a finite verb, *does answer*. A comma sets off the clause. In example b, the first word could be either a subordinating conjunction or a simple preposition. Because the group of words it introduces, *after the fourth ring*, is a phrase without both subject and finite verb, no comma is needed.

An exception to this rule about introductory clauses and phrases is that if the introductory group of words is long or syntactically complex, it should be set off with a comma whether it is a clause or a phrase.

> Example: *Without the right tool for the task, Morris had to rely on his pocket knife.*

Another exception to the rule is made for sentence modifiers, mentioned in guideline 14d.

> Example: *Under the circumstances, you should expect a sizable crowd and be prepared to answer questions.*

> Example: *Nevertheless, the action you choose now will affect all future decisions.*

Whether the introductory modifier is long or short, if it modifies the sentence as a whole, and not just the verb, it is set off. Compare the treatment of *therefore* in the following passages.

Example: *The dog was prowling the backyard fence.*
Therefore, the cat remained close to the house.

Example: *The former athlete had a metal pin in his left*
knee. He therefore walked with a slight limp.

The writer of the first example punctuates *therefore* as a
sentence modifier. The writer of the second example treats
therefore as an adverb modifying *walks.*

The most common use of commas to separate is in a
series.

Example: *Commas are used for linking, separating, and*
enclosing.

The rule is the same whether the elements in a series are
single words, phrases, or clauses.

Example: *Commas are used for linking, for separating, and*
for enclosing.

Example: *Commas are used for linking clauses in a sen-*
tence, for separating items in a series, and for enclos-
ing parenthetical information.

Example: *Commas link clauses in a sentence, they sepa-*
rate items in a series, and they enclose parenthetical
information.

If the items in a series have internal commas, the
commas that separate the items are normally replaced
with semicolons to avoid confusion. The opening sentence
of this section on commas is such a sentence:

Commas are used for three purposes: linking, as
between clauses in a sentence; separating, as between
items in a series; and enclosing, as in setting off paren-
thetical information.

The only doubtful aspect of the rule about items in a series is whether to include a comma before the *and* or *or* that introduces the last item in the series. Most current authorities favor including the comma even before the *and* to avoid possible confusion. The following sentence will illustrate:

> *The oldest buildings on the street are those that house Fidelity Corporation, the insurance company of Burkes and Avery and Comminger.*

Without a comma to separate the second and third elements in this series, we cannot tell whether *Avery* is part of the insurance company *Burkes and Avery* or whether the last item in the series is a company called *Avery and Comminger*.

To eliminate possible confusion, it is necessary to include a comma before *and* in any series that includes *and* as part of one of the items in series. Having made that decision, for consistency a writer should include a comma before the *and* in every series.

When several adjective modifiers precede a noun, commas may be used to separate the adjectives. Notice the differences among the following sentences:

Example a: *the old, weathered, and cracking paint must be removed before a new coat is applied.*

Example b: *An abandoned, empty railroad car squats on the siding behind the station.*

Example c: *The rustle of her bright blue, freshly starched dress attracted attention as she walked to the front of the room.*

In example a, the three adjectives are essentially equal modifiers, lined up in a series. They must be separated by commas. In example b, *abandoned* is separated from *empty* by a comma because they are essentially equivalent, but both adjectives modify *railroad car* as a single unit. Therefore *railroad* is not set off. In example c, *bright* modifies *blue*, *freshly* modifies *starched*. The punctuation reflects this structure.

A variation of the rule governing punctuation of adjectives holds that if the three modifiers are lined up from general to specific, commas are not needed.

Example d: *The stage was decorated with lovely fresh white flowers.*

16c.   Use commas to enclose.

Commas are used to enclose material that is interruptive or parenthetical in force. In the next section we will return to parenthetical elements and the other ways of enclosing them, with dashes and parentheses, but the most common way of signaling interruptive or parenthetical words or phrases is with commas.

Sometimes the material enclosed is clearly parenthetical:

Example: *It was, believe me, God's gift of a day.*

Example: *The project will be completed, according to our estimate, two weeks before the deadline specified in the contract.*

Modifying clauses and phrases are not always seen as parenthetical. They are more or less parenthetical, depending on how closely they are linked to the words they modify. Editors and grammarians make a useful distinction between restrictive and nonrestrictive modifiers. Restrictive modifiers provide essential, identifying information about the words they modify. Nonrestrictive modifiers provide additional but non-identifying information. The comma rule is that restrictive modifiers are not set off by commas; nonrestrictive modifiers are.

> Example, restrictive: *This motion will identify the errors that the commission made so that the agency may correct them or prepare to defend them on appeal.*

> Example, nonrestrictive: *Our company operates six of these wider trailers, which are known as "super-wides," on the interstate highways in Texas.*

In the first example, *that the commission made* identifies the errors in question. Because the clause is necessary to identify the errors, the clause is restrictive. In the second example, *which are known as "super-wides"* provides additional information not needed to identify the type of trailers. The clause is nonrestrictive, parenthetical in effect; it must be enclosed in commas. Notice that the nonrestrictive modifier in the second example is a nonrestrictive clause. It would be nonrestrictive even if it were a phrase. It would be punctuated as follows:

> *Our company operates six of these wider trailers, known as "super-wides," on the interstate highways of Texas.*

A corollary rule governing restrictive and nonrestrictive clauses—that restrictive relative clauses are introduced by *that*, nonrestrictive relative clauses are introduced by *which* (see guideline 10b)—may help you distinguish between restrictive and nonrestrictive clauses. If a modifying clause begins with *that*, we can expect no comma before the clause; if a modifying clause begins with *which*, the clause will likely be set off. Unfortunately, anyone having trouble distinguishing between restrictive and nonrestrictive clauses will also have trouble knowing whether to use *which* or *that*. Moreover, the rule governing the selection of *which* or *that* is often superseded by other stylistic considerations. Consider the following example:

> We have learned that packages that are delivered by that service frequently arrive damaged.

The three instances of *that* in one short sentence scream for revision. One way to revise would be to override the rule requiring *that* to introduce a restrictive modifier:

> We have learned that packages which are delivered by that service frequently arrive damaged.

The sentence could be further modified:

> We have learned that packages delivered by Jiffy Mail frequently arrive damaged.

However the sentence is revised, the clause or phrase modifying *packages* is restrictive.

Two other hints will help you to identify restrictive and nonrestrictive modifiers. The first has to do with the way we read restrictive and nonrestrictive modifiers.

Example a: *Christina attends a school that groups two grades together in a single classroom.*

Example b: *This school, in existence since 1974, was designed to offer continuous progress for all its students.*

Notice that in reading example a aloud you would probably not pause after *school*. Because the modifier that follows is essential and identifies the school, there is no pause and therefore no comma. In example b, however, a reader would normally pause slightly after *school* and again after *1974* because the nonrestrictive phrase is felt as parenthetical. The pauses are reflected by the commas.

The rhythm of reading aloud is personal and may vary

from reader to reader. Listening for the pauses, therefore, is not a sure way to identify nonrestrictive modifiers.

The other hint is to test whether the relative pronoun, *which* or *that*, can be omitted without damaging the sentence. This test only works with a relative pronoun that is not the subject of its clause.

> Example a: *The booklet that you will find in your packet includes instructions for arranging your materials.*

> Example b: *These procedures, which we have tested with several teams, will provide for safe and efficient handling of the cargo.*

Notice in example *a*, *that* can be omitted without affecting the sense or readability of the sentence. The clause following *booklet* is restrictive. In example *b*, removing *which* would result in some confusion. The clause following *procedures* is nonrestrictive.

Once the restrictive/nonrestrictive distinction is mastered, the remaining occasions for enclosing words and phrases in commas will seem easy. **Conjunctive adverbs** and other transitional words and phrases that occur within a sentence are normally set off, enclosed in commas. The examples will make clear what we mean by conjunctive adverbs and transitional words and phrases.

> Example, conjunctive adverb: *The evidence, however, is persuasive.*

> Example, conjunctive adverb: *It may be true, nevertheless, that all students graduating from the same high school have the same academic credits.*

A short list of conjunctive adverbs will establish the category rather firmly.

CONJUNCTIVE ADVERBS

however	*obviously*
moreover	*consequently*
incidentally	*fortunately*
nevertheless	*instead*
furthermore	

Other phrases that interrupt in the same way, but are less frequent in their occurrence, should be treated in the same way.

   Example, transitional phrase: *The reasons are, after all, fairly obvious.*

   Example, transitional phrase: *A large box, on the other hand, may hold so many books it can't be lifted.*

The distinction between conjunctive adverbs and other transitional phrases is only conventional and hardly clean. The only real difference is whether the interrupting element contains one word or several. In either case, the interrupting element is set off by commas.

   Another construction that can be treated as parenthetical is the **appositive phrase.**

   Example a: *My cousin, a police officer, wears a uniform nearly every day.*

   Example b: *Hilda's knee injury required a specialist, an orthopedic surgeon.*

In each of these examples, a noun phrase modifies and renames the noun immediately before it. The modifying phrase is an appositive. It might be labeled as an elliptical nonrestrictive clause—*who is a police officer* or *who was an orthopedic surgeon.* Clause, phrase, or single word, the modifier is parenthetical in force and is set off by commas.

Titles and labels for persons are regarded as appositives if they follow the names but not if they precede the names.

Example: *My sister Emma Granger will arrive by bus.*

Example: *Emma Granger, my sister, will arrive by bus.*

Example: *George Babbitt, president of the Zenith Chamber of Commerce, chairs our Board of Trustees.*

Example: *President George Babbitt of the Zenith Chamber of Commerce chairs our Board of Trustees.*

Example: *Zenith Chamber of Commerce president George Babbitt chairs our Board of Trustees.*

When one or more nonrestrictive modifiers (sometimes called free modifiers) follow the **subject-predicate** nucleus of a clause, the trailing modifiers are set off from the base clause and from each other by commas.

Example a: *In the last decade especially, paleoanthropology has hardened itself as a science, developing ever-more-precise methods and greatly expanding the mass of evidence that lies at its roots.*

[Lucy's Child, p. 31]

Example b: *The main clause, which may or may not have a sentence modifier before it, advances the discussion; but the additions move backward, as in this clause, to modify the statement of the main clause or more often to explicate or exemplify it, so that the sentence has a flowing and ebbing movement, advancing to a new position and then pausing to consolidate it, leaping and lingering as the popular ballad does.*

[Notes toward a New Rhetoric, pp. 27–28]

Example a illustrates free modifiers following the base clause, set off with a comma. Because the two modifiers are parallel, they are not separated. Example b, from a book on style, was constructed specifically to illustrate the principle it explains.

We have covered most of the essential rules of punctuation. It may be helpful to summarize the rules governing commas before we go on to talk of exceptions and special punctuation rules.

SUMMARY OF COMMA RULES

- For linking independent clauses in a compound sentence, use a comma and a coordinating conjunction. The comma goes before the conjunction.
- Use a comma to set off an introductory clause, but use a comma after an introductory phrase only if it is long or if it is a sentence modifier.
- Use commas between elements in a series, including a comma before the *and* or *or* that introduces the last item in the series.
- Use commas to enclose material that is interruptive or parenthetical, including nonrestrictive clauses or phrases, conjunctive adverbs, appositive words or phrases, and trailing free modifiers.

The list, as you can see, is surprisingly short. Although each of these rules requires some practice to apply it well, any serious writer should be able to master the standard rules with ease.

One additional word of advice about commas: unless you have a reason to put in a comma, don't. Most writers go astray in punctuating their work by adding commas where they are not needed. If the rules do not tell you to put in a comma, you are better off without it.

Punctuation Beyond the Essentials

I suggested in the summary essay for this chapter that we attend to the placement of commas during the editing and revision stage of writing. Making the necessary allowance that we pay attention to composing and editing simultaneously during most writing, I want to introduce some punctuation marks that should be considered a resource for composing rather than a checklist for editing. These are punctuation marks with their own syntactic force, marks that allow a writer to say some things that wouldn't be possible otherwise.

17. Use a colon to cast forward.

The colon has specific uses that, when properly understood, can streamline writing and manage information. In current editing practice a colon is roughly equivalent to the phrase, "as follows."

> Example: *Any self-contained vehicle must have at least three elements: a power source, wheels or some other device to deliver the power, and a space for carrying the load.*

The colon eliminates the need to put a period after *elements* and add the words, *they are.* In many situations we can use the syntactic force of the colon to bring ideas together.

> Example: *The representative should carry all her supplies: a sample case, brochures explaining the product, and order blanks.*

In using the colon, however, it is important to avoid certain pitfalls. A colon is not for use just any time a series is to follow. It is not proper to put a colon between a verb and its object or between a preposition and its object.

Example: *The billiard ball hit: an end cushion, another ball, a second cushion, and the pocket.*

Correction: *The billiard ball hit an end cushion, another ball, a second cushion, and the pocket.*

Example: *I would like to be transferred to: Tucson, Boston, or Miami.*

Correction: *I would like to be transferred to Tucson, Boston, or Miami.*

Either sentence is incorrect with a colon. What comes before a colon should be a complete grammatical unit that makes sense without the series. What comes after the colon should be a complete unit that renames or specifies what is mentioned before.

Example: *The writer is faced with two separate but related tasks: gathering correct information and finding a form in which to present the information.*

The point to be emphasized here is that the colon is not a decorative mark added after the fact. Because of its real function in the grammar of a sentence, the colon should be used and manipulated as a part of the language.

18. Use a dash to cast back.

Another mark of punctuation, a partner to the colon and making a contrastive pair, is the dash—made in typed manuscripts with a double hyphen. Whereas the colon is most often used before a series, the dash commonly appears after a series.

Example: *Accuracy, versatility, and speed—these are the qualities we look for in a processor.*

The colon directs our attention forward; the dash directs our attention backward.

A single dash is also used in the middle of a sentence when the sentence is interrupted and starts in a new direction.

Example: *My daughter Edna has moved to Portland—she's married now, you know.*

This use of the dash is more common in creative writing or informal correspondence than it is in technical or business communications. Used sparingly, however, it is not out of place in formal writing.

Perhaps a more common use of dashes is in pairs of dashes that function roughly as parentheses do. If the writer wants to insert an aside or perhaps add a comment on what the text says, a pair of dashes will set that comment apart.

Example: *You will receive our shipment—we have a letter of confirmation—as soon as the carrier service is restored.*

Example: *Our representative in your area—she is one of our most experienced analysts—will be there Monday to talk with your employees.*

There are three ways of setting such parenthetical matter off within a sentence: a pair of commas, a pair of dashes, and parentheses. Notice the differences among the following examples:

Example a: *The third pamphlet in our series, which will be published next month, will be more technical in content.*

Example b: *When we are ready for a church organ—every church needs an organ—we will launch another fund-raising campaign.*

Example c: *At last the green chair (you remember that green overstuffed chair in the back room) has gone to the shop to be re-covered.*

In example a the parenthetical phrase is a nonrestrictive modifier, only slightly parenthetical. In b and c, the phrases are more clearly parenthetical. Just how parenthetical is a matter of individual judgment. A writer might exchange parentheses and dashes between the two sample sentences, b and c.

One word of advice about paired dashes and parentheses: don't overuse the device. The effect achieved by paired dashes or by parentheses loses its force quickly. The writer who overuses this or any other unconventional punctuation strategy risks the charge of affectation. The moment the punctuation becomes noticeable for its own sake, the message takes a second-place position. Good punctuation is nearly transparent.

19. Use a semicolon to manage main clauses and complex series.

The last mark I want to consider is the semicolon. According to a manuscript convention observed a hundred years ago, the semicolon signaled a major pause within a sentence, in magnitude somewhere between a comma and a period. Modern editorial practice circumscribes uses of the semicolon more specifically. The principal use of the semicolon is between the clauses of a compound sentence. If you use a semicolon, no conjunction is required.

Example a: *Our team will be in your city on Friday; we will call from the airport.*

Example b: *Our sales have improved dramatically; we have opened two new branches.*

The rhetorical advantage of the semicolon is precisely that it links the clauses in a compound sentence without requiring a conjunction. Used correctly, the semicolon can be a device of great subtlety. In example b, it is not clear whether the branches have been opened because sales have improved or whether sales have improved because two new branches have been added. The context would no doubt make the meaning clear. The manager writing the sentence compliments the intelligence of the sales force by letting the readers make the connection.

The other most common use of the semicolon has already been covered, to separate elements of a series when one or more elements have commas within them.

Purely Conventional Punctuation

Even after the writer is in control of periods and commas, after the writer has mastered such specialized marks as dashes and semicolons, situations remain that every writer encounters daily, situations that require a command of purely conventional punctuation rules. Some of these rules make good sense grammatically; some are historical relics of earlier times. There are two ways to master these rules. The simpler but less efficient way is to keep a handbook by your side and look them up whenever questions arise. The better way is to use and reuse them often enough that they become deeply practiced, nearly reflexive behaviors. There is no simpler way to present them than as a list of rules to be learned.

20.　Place a comma or a period inside quotation marks.

Example: *Our class enjoyed reading the short story, "Paul's Case."*

Example: *After saying, "class dismissed," the teacher walked to the back of the room.*

When any other mark of punctuation coincides with the end of a title or quoted passage, the logic of the situation determines whether the punctuation mark goes inside or outside the quotation marks.

Example: *Do you have this recording of "God Bless America"?*

Example: *The child's question, "Where is my mom?" brought tears to the police officer's eyes.*

At the end of any syntactic unit—a phrase, a clause, or a sentence—use only one mark of punctuation, whether there are quotation marks or not.

Example: *The child left the stage after singing her song, "Where's Johnny?"*

Example: *The professor's full title is written, "Eduard Ramon, Ph.D."*

Although the first example is not a question, the question mark in the title ends the sentence. In the second example, the period after *D* serves the double function of indicating the abbreviation and ending the sentence.

21. Place parentheses inside a punctuation mark, except with complete sentences.

Example: *The sailor arrived home on December 3 (his birthday).*

Example: *For many experienced writers (myself included), the editing stage is the most challenging.*

It is not unusual for a complete sentence intended as parenthetical to keep its punctuation inside the parentheses.

Example: *I have added my comments to those already written on the manuscript. (My pencil is purple.)*

The following example comes from a book of informal philosophy. Its use of parentheses and other punctuation devices marks it as informal.

> *One night I stood beside him at the wedging board while he morosely kneaded and slapped his clay. Suddenly he spoke. "What is a potter?" His accomplishment meant nothing to him. He did not LIKE his pots. They bore no individual stamp, he said. They did not speak to him. (Perhaps he had not spoken to them?) "What should a potter do?" he asked me. What should he make? Who should a potter be? (You see these are real questions that men do ask!)*

[Centering, p. 26]

Notice that the author breaks with convention in other ways, using a word in all capital letters, a question mark where no question is intended, and an exclamation point inside a parenthetical remark. Such departures would not be appropriate for a formal paper or business report.

22.   In dates, addresses, and titles, place commas before and after the second and subsequent elements.

Example a: *The Interstate that runs through Fort Worth, Texas, has the same number as the Interstate in Minneapolis, Minnesota.*

Example b: *On December 7, 1941, the Japanese air force attacked Pearl Harbor.*

Example c: *James C. Watson, Lieutenant Colonel, U.S. Army (retired), will attend the ceremony at the state capital.*

23.   Avoid strategies of spelling or punctuation to add emphasis.

If you feel the need to underline words or spell them in all capital letters to give them added punch, you probably need to rewrite the passage so that it will carry sufficient emphasis. Excessive use of any punctuation strategy, from exclamation points to parentheses, will draw attention away from the message.

A bit of related advice: it is wise to avoid quotation marks, sometimes called "scare quotes," around words that seem out of place.

Example a: *Our supervisor is a "student" of banking principles.*

Example b: *The students in my class were "blown away" by the movie version of* Death of a Salesman.

The author of each of these sentences betrays some insecurity about using a term in an unorthodox context. In each case the writer would be on surer ground leaving the words alone, not calling attention to them with quotation marks. If the writer is uncomfortable using these words, it is better to select other words.

24.   Be careful with apostrophes, hyphens, and italics.

The most common use of the apostrophe ['] is to replace omitted letters in a contraction or to indicate the possessive (what grammarians call the **genitive case**).

Example, contraction: *I'll be curious to see how your work develops.*

Example, possessive: *By a little winding staircase we climbed to the second floor of Pablo's apartment.*

The first part of the rule governing possessives is, for singular words add *'s.* This part of the rule applies even if the singular word ends in *s.*

Example: *Mr. Jones's gate is higher than Douglas's car.*

When the word is long and ends in an *s,* some writers use the apostrophe without adding another *s.*

Example: *Massachusetts' population is greater than Connecticut's.*

A careful writer, however, would probably recast the sentence to avoid the cumbersome possessive form.

Correction: *The population of Massachusetts is greater than that of Connecticut.*

The rest of the rule is, for plural words that end in *s,* add only *'*; if the plural ends in a different letter, add *'s.*

Example a: *The two dogs' collars have the same ornate pattern.*

Example b: *Underneath the table I saw the men's suits folded up.*

The rule governing the formation of possessives is somewhat intricate, but it seldom causes problems for writers. The most frequent error writing students make is forming the plural with an apostrophe. If the word is not possessive, do not use an apostrophe.

Another situation likely to cause indecision is making plurals of Arabic numbers or of letters.

Example: *The decade of the 1960s was a period of social change.*

Example: *Mary Ellen made two B's in her first semester of college.*

Authorities disagree about whether to use apostrophes in making plurals of numbers and letters that are not full words. It is best to avoid the apostrophe when making plurals of numbers. But letters made plural without the apostrophe may be confusing. Notice how the following might be confused:

> Example: *I find the Model As appealing.*

> Example: *We all encounter Bs sooner or later.*

The presence of hyphens in most words is a matter of spelling and can be resolved with a dictionary. Surprisingly few words have hyphens in their normal spelling.

> Example: *The child found her jack-in-the-box behind the door.*

A hyphen joins two words used as a single modifier.

> Example: *On a two-day trip across the country we traveled by plane and train.*

If the modifier is made up of an adjective and one or more modifiers, however, the modifying phrase contains no hyphens.

> Example: *The bright blue painting is an attractive addition to our office.*

> Example: *The slowly closing door blocked her view of the inner room.*

The most important rule about hyphens is, use them sparingly.

Words used out of context and foreign words are conventionally underlined or set in italic type, depending on the capabilities of the typewriter or the word processor.

> Example: *The conjunction <u>and</u> is more often misused than any other word I can think of.*

Example: *The real impediments to an effective performance are fatigue and ennui.*

The rule governing terms from other languages is difficult to apply consistently because English adopts foreign words so easily. We can hardly say whether *hacienda* is Spanish or English. Most of us would use *eskimo* without underlining or italics; however, we would probably underline the French spelling, *esquimau*, even though it is the same word spelled differently.

The other most common use of underlining and italics is in giving the titles of books or other works of art. In business situations and in many publications the conventions for listing titles are flexible.

Example: *This calm, monumental figure, enveloped in atmosphere, is a preparatory study for the epoch-making painting,* La Grande Jatte.
[Modern Prints and Drawings, p. 45]

Example: *In "Guernica" and kindred works, rage against brutality produced figures, outlined to the last tooth, distorted to symbolize the real-life nightmare of total war.*
[The Drawings of Picasso, p. 2]

Book editors usually prefer underlining or italics for titles of works that stand alone. For letters and reports the important principle is to be consistent.

For students writing papers in college or any other academic context, a mastery of the conventions of citation form is crucial. Different disciplines, however, use different forms for citation, each with its own way of ordering the information and each with its own punctuation rules. For that reason this guide offers no method for notes and citations. The college writer is advised to consult the instructor of each course, learn the name of the correct manual for the discipline of the course (*MLA, APA, Math into Type,* and so on), and follow the manual carefully.

EXERCISES

Essentials

15.   Punctuate the end of a sentence with a period, a question mark, or an exclamation point.

Directions: Punctuate the following sentences. You may need to make more than one sentence, or you may need to combine sentences.

1. Thank you for attending our banquet for the retiring staff members

2. Congratulations I was pleased to see an employee of DataCorp win the award

3. How generous you are I will treasure your gift

4. I want to know if you have finished the report you were working on

5. What kind of loyalty is this when an employee walks out after twelve years for the first offer that comes along

6. Stop your bickering I can't stand distractions when I am working

7. Tell me how do you plan to respond to the institute's request

8. He doesn't understand why he has to remind his wife to plan their anniversary after all that's her responsibility not his

9. Where are the volunteers I want to know

10. It's no longer a question of who will manage the

accounts it is now an issue of who will make company policy

11. The story of Chief Joseph and his doomed people raises many questions Why did the U.S. Army insist on treating the Indians the way it did were the white settlers justified in taking the Indians territory

12. The health care system of this country is a staggering enterprise in any sense of the adjective whatever the failures of distribution and lack of coordination it is the gigantic scale and scope of the total collective effort that first catches the breath and the cost [The Medusa and the Snail, p. 36]

16. Follow the rules governing commas.

Directions: Some of the sentences in this exercise have no punctuation; some have punctuation in the wrong places; some are correct. Edit for punctuation.

1. This year because of the larger enrollments. We are offering the course at several times.

2. We have many pairs of skates but none in your size

3. Chief Joseph was a peaceful honorable man who loved his land and his people.

4. Although the examples in this exercise are crafted for the occasion they could as easily have been drawn from published sources.

5. After the glamor of traveling to exotic locales how will she adjust to the ordinary day by day of a home office job.

6. Under the new regulations we will not be able to use the application form we used to.

7. The asters comprise a very large genus there being more than 650 species from nearly all parts of the world except Australia. [Roadside Flowers of Texas, p. 228]

8. Our report is not ready because we were unable to complete the telephone survey as scheduled in May.

9. Course offerings vary from site to site, they include a self paced individualized sequence covering arithmetic/pre-algebra/algebra reading the classics basics of writing Latin for language development mathematical problem solving and science exploration. [Flexible Pacing for Able Learners, p. 57]

10. We start with the belief that the best education takes place when new concepts new content are presented in a way and at a pace that fits diverse learning rates and learning styles.

11. In fact his foolish behavior could land him in court

12. Fortunately today more and more people are aware of the benefits of recycling, however some Neanderthals will always clog our landfills with reusable paper and cans.

13. Among Dalworth National and Lane, Sewell ranks Dalworth first in terms of revenue paid for transportation. Among Dalworth Lane and National—National is used least because of a history of late deliveries equipment not being available and Sewells perception that on time deliveries are not important to National.

14. The absence of any evidence showing that the grant of these applications would cause hardship to competitors or interfere with services which they are now rendering presents good cause to grant these applications.

15. Particularly at those schools where scheduling has been arranged in blocks to permit an easy flow of students from group to group studying the same subject at different levels the abler students have found a more steady challenge and less repetition. [Flexible Pacing for Able Learners, p. 97]

16. Junior college commissioner Dr. Lawrence Keating

has announced a capital campaign county-wide to run from September 1991 through May 1992

17. This trend resulting in a 3% increase in sales for the third quarter is expected to continue for at least two years.

18. John Elliot my former teacher has bought a home in your neighborhood.

Punctuation Beyond the Essentials

17–19.   Use a colon to cast forward, a dash to cast back, and a semicolon to manage main clauses and complex series.

Directions: Provide helpful punctuation for the following sentences. You may need to recast some sentences.

1. The next few pages describe an investment that we believe embodies these objectives, an investment that combines income with tax benefits, that has historically performed well, that will fit in comfortably with your present investment portfolio, an investment which exhibits real potential to increase in value.

2. In her essay "In Search of Our Mothers' Gardens," Alice Walker includes: outrage balanced by sympathy, reverence set against disgust—examples of contrasting emotional tones.

3. What they fear is what most people want a secure home, a regular schedule, rules that have some meaning.

4. On his return to Paris in 1822 two years before his untimely death Géricault produced some of his finest and most influential pictures:—the group of drawings lithographs and watercolors of race and work horses and an unforgettable series of realistic haunting portraits of insane people. [Modern Prints and Drawings, p. 8]

5. Why are the business applications of graphics growing so fast. There are two main reasons lower hardware and software prices, and the advances in computer graphics technology.

6. Driving out of the beleaguered city into the suburbs is immediately to encounter a different happier world, a prosperous middle-class place that knows no violence; big comfortable houses built to sustain and celebrate the simple happiness of family life. [Wilson, Sins and All, p. 1]

7. Life leads us at a certain moment to step beyond the dualisms to which we have been educated, primitive and civilized chaos and order abnormal and normal private and public verbal and nonverbal conventional and far-out good and bad.

8. This guide is for people in industry who regularly write reports and proposals memos and business letters. They are counselors and architects public administrators surveyors lawyers and commercial artists, professionals who must communicate with clients and associates clearly and directly. [Guide, p. 5]

9. The hardest part this was no picnic I assure you was rechecking each address to be sure that no client had been listed incorrectly.

10. In practical terms the scoring depends on the disposition of the judges and that says it all.

11. The author regards this as typical adolescent behavior however, I think the young woman is justified in feeling abandoned.

12. First of all Virginia Woolfe's essay, "Professions for Women" gives the reader a sense of hearing the author in person; not just reading from a page.

13. Elsewhere honesty may be the best policy in research it is the only policy.

14. Stated topic sentences often appear somewhere near the beginning of a paragraph as in the first paragraph of this chapter, they can also appear at the end or even in the middle of a paragraph. [Writing for the 21st-Century, p. 162]

15. My grades were as follows two As in economics and history two Bs in accounting and chemistry and a C in my only elective History of Dance.

Purely Conventional Punctuation

Refer to guidelines 20–24.

Directions: Provide any needed punctuation. You may need to change the punctuation provided.

1. The mans attitude toward sex roles comes right out of "Genesis".

2. The females lighter skeleton and her muscle structure suit her better than a man for some athletic activities

3. Next summer Dr. White will offer his new course "Artist of the Century": Picasso and 20th-Century Art it will focus on our centuries most influential artist.

4. Exhibit 50 which is a survey of shipments during November, 1989 shows the shipper and location number of loads for each shipper and whether the load was delivered "on time" "late" or "unknown".

5. All this makes Judith seem more like an actual person, and makes it easier to sympathize, and to respond emotionally to what she suffers: we feel just how unjust it is and how tragic for such a "gifted" young woman (or any young woman) to come to such a fate.

6. Several lineages of the earliest humanlike primates had evolved by about five million years ago. Among them were two Australopithecines (southern apes): the large Australopithecus robustus and the much smaller Australopithecus africanus. [Humankind, p. 40]

7. On May 5 1990 a major fund raising drive was launched in Austin Texas at the university law school.

8. That was the situation when the council began its campaign with the slogan Pick up with pride.

9. The magazine Aura is running a series of articles on the woman of the '90's as perceived by business leaders in the community.

10. "I am a little bit of a woman" Harriet Beecher Stowe wrote of herself in 1853 "somewhat more than 40 about as thin and dry as a piece of snuff". [Life, Special Report, p. 37]

Combining Punctuation Marks

The true test of punctuation skill is in larger contexts, contexts that provide some range of punctuation options. Punctuate these paragraphs in a way that makes sense to you. You may need to capitalize letters or convert capitals to lower case. Some punctuation has been provided, but it may be misleading.

1. Rarely in recent memory have people been faced with so much uncertainty when attempting to develop a successful investment strategy The unsettled state of the economy The enormous impact of taxes The disarray of the Social Security system and the distressing lack of consensus among experts as to which direction the economy is actually headed raise serious questions about relying on traditional forms of investment. For investors seeking income the bewildering and ever-changing number of investment choices, money market funds bank certificates, savings and loan accounts bonds dividend-paying stocks, only add to the confusion Where can individuals turn, Which investments make the most sense today What should you look for in the income investments you choose. [QUIP II investment brochure]

2. My friends generally dropped out of school. Many of them close during my elementary school years no longer have an academic future, simply refused the challenge and accepted the ways of the street. I saw this as losing at the game we all must play. A game of chance that only those with extraordinary determination can be successful at. [Student paper]

3. What I want to say is that as our personal universes expand if we keep drawing ourselves into center again and again everything seems to enhance everything else. It becomes unnecessary to choose which person to be as we open and close the same ball of clay. We will make pots for our English classes. Read poems to our pottery classes. Write on the clay, print from the clay. The activity seems to spring out of the same source poem or pot loaf of bread letter to a friend a mornings meditation a walk in the woods turning the compost pile knitting a pair of shoes weeping with pain fainting with discouragement burning with shame trembling with indecision what's the difference. I like especially two famous Zen stories the one about the great Japanese master of the art of archery who had never in his life hit the bulls eye. And the other about the monk who said Now that I'm enlightened I'm just as miserable as ever. [Centering, p. 23]

4. I want to repeat that this book is a guide not a set of rules. If you find that following a guideline would make your writing sound unnatural ignore the guideline for example the guide suggests you avoid passive constructions, yet in some situations the passive sounds right. If it sounds right it probably is, in the final analysis the best writing sounds natural. One purpose behind these guide-lines is to help you train your ear so that crisp tight prose will sound right, the other purpose is to encourage you to trust your own judgment. [Guide, p. 5]

5. The town of Lake Wobegon Minnesota lies on the shore against Adams Hill looking east across the blue-green water to the dark woods, from the south the high-way aims for the lake bends hard left by the magnificent Grecian grain silos and eases over a leg of the hill past the slow children sign bringing the traveler in on Main Street toward the towns one traffic light which is almost always green. Along the ragged dirt path between the asphalt and the grass a child slowly walks to Ralphs Grocery kick-ing an asphalt chunk ahead of him, it is a chunk that after four blocks he is now mesmerized by to which he is completely dedicated. At Bunsen Motors the sidewalk begins a breeze off the lake brings a sweet air of mud and rotting wood a slight fishy smell and picks up the sweet-ness of the old grease a sharp whiff of gasoline fresh tires spring dust and from across the street the faint essence of tuna hotdish from the Chatterbox Cafe. [Lake Wobegon Days, pp. 1–2]

Chapter Four

Avoiding Sexist Language

SUMMARY ESSAY

In classrooms and in board rooms, at committee meetings, strategy sessions, and political caucuses—wherever people talk about writing persuasive prose, they eventually talk about avoiding sexist language, or, more positively, using inclusive language. The topic stirs emotions both among those who welcome the changes in our language and among those who believe the hoo-rah is silly. My students say to me, "But I've always been taught to use masculine pronouns when both sexes are intended. My teacher told me *man* is a generic noun and includes women as well as men."

"Not any more," I reply.

"Using *he/she* and substituting *person* for *man* every time—that's so awkward and unnatural."

I agree.

This chapter makes two points. The first is that no writer can ignore the sexist bias inherent in our language. None of us is responsible for the conventions that have dominated our language for centuries. But we are accountable for how we use the language today. Writers at all levels and in any business or social context must confront the need to include all their readers in everything they write. The second point of this chapter is that using inclusive language well requires more than simply substituting *he/she* wherever the masculine form appears. Frequently a writer has to reconstruct a sentence or a whole passage to make the communication more inclusive and at the same time make the writing sound natural and direct.

Before beginning I must say something about terminology. The words used to label the differences between men and women remain unsettled. At one end of the scale, in talking about biological functions, *sex* is appropriate and the classes are *male* and *female.* At the other end of the scale, where grammar is the issue, *gender* is the correct term, and the distinction is between *masculine* and *feminine.* The pronouns of feminine gender are *she, her,* and *hers;* the masculine pronouns are *he, him* and *his.* For discussion of the culturally determined roles in society and ways we respond to men and women, the choice is not clear. Francine Wattman Frank and Paula Treichler make a convincing case for using *gender* to designate the cultural and other attributes identified with each sex.

Because my topic is primarily language, I am strict about using *gender* for masculine and feminine grammatical classes. In describing social and cultural roles, I mix *sex* and *gender,* choosing whichever word seems to fit best. My chief goal is to make the presentation clear.

With that distinction out of the way, let me start with some of the reasons for using inclusive language. In academic papers or in writing for the workplace, the challenge to avoid sexist language is persistent and nagging. Our readers will notice if we write, "Man is an animal who laughs." They will want to know if we intended to imply that women have no sense of humor. If a manager writes, "Each employee must have his file updated annually," someone in the office will wonder if female employees are subject to the same rule. None of us can claim we intended to incorporate both sexes, or we assumed everyone would understand. The language conventions have changed. If we mean to include men and women equally, we must do so explicitly.

In academic writing the requirement to use inclusive language is virtually universal. I can illustrate with two brief excerpts from official academic publications. In its *Guidelines for Nonsexist Use of Language in NCTE Publications* (revised, 1985), the National Council of Teachers of English takes the following position:

> These guidelines for nonsexist language are suggestions for teachers, writers, and contributors to NCTE publications. For the editors of NCTE publications, however, they are a statement of policy.

The stand announced in the Third Edition of the *Publication Manual of the American Psychological Association* (1983) is similar:

> In 1982 the APA Publications and Communications Board adopted a policy that requires authors who are submitting their manuscripts to an APA journal to use nonsexist language, that is, to avoid in their manuscripts language that could be construed as sexist.

College students learning to write for the professions they hope to enter have little choice. They must acquire the strategies to avoid sexist language.

For those in the workplace, the issue takes on a slightly different cast. Good marketing sense and the politics of the workplace require writers in business to avoid offending clients and customers. For such writers the task is to insure that their writing includes all who are affected by what they write.

The reasons for using inclusive language go beyond a personal philosophy. Inclusive language is expected in all public contexts. Writers need to know that. Every good writer should be able to avoid sexist language completely and artfully. It is not easy; for many of us, avoiding sexist language means retraining.

Writing inclusively requires two kinds of choices. While composing we must select words and images that do not depend on or reinforce sex-role or gender stereotypes profoundly embedded in our culture. Choices made while editing help us catch more superficial but equally damaging instances of sexist language.

To illustrate careless thinking embedded in thoughtless generalizations, I quote two paragraphs from a pamphlet on selling techniques prepared by a life insurance office:

> The progress of civilization, to a great extent, has been the result of men selling to other men the idea that their products or services would lead to a better life. Salesmanship has been practiced since one caveman convinced another that he would be better off to trade his stone axe for a stone spearhead. Salesmanship was used by the Phoenicians and Greeks as they sailed the Mediterranean in search of buyers for their oils and perfumes.
>
> A hermit is about the only person in our society today whose well-being does not depend, to some extent, upon the daily use of salesmanship. As a normal human being, you have used and will use salesmanship from the cradle to the grave:
>
> 1. As a baby, you cried to get what you wanted.
> 2. As a child, you sold your dad on taking you to the circus.
> 3. As a college boy, you sold your father on your new life style.
> 4. As an adult, when you finished school, you sold yourself to an employer.
> 5. As a businessman, you continually sell yourself to your associates.
> 6. At retirement, you may sell your wife on the desirability of moving to Florida, California, or the West Indies.
>
> [Life insurance brochure]

The writer of this pamphlet thinks of its audience as entirely male. But the exclusive language is so heavy that it suggests the writer was consciously writing to keep women out of the industry.

It may be unfair to make my point with an exaggerated example. The following paragraph comes from a writing manual published in 1975 by the engineering division of a defense contractor. In his preface to the manual, the male author refers to technical writers using masculine pronouns exclusively:

> But the true measure of the guide's success does not lie with its author; it lies with its user. He not only must read the guide but also must apply what he has read. And he must apply it everywhere, every time he writes—and even when he reads, because much about writing can be learned from studying and questioning how the other fellow uses it.
>
> [Guide to Achieving Style, p. v]

The writer of this manual might step forward to argue that the masculine pronouns are used generically, that they include all writers, male and female. But the final clause, "how the other fellow uses it," establishes that in the author's mind all technical writers (perhaps all writers) are male.

The examples could be multiplied. In a prospectus offering limited partnerships as a form of investment, a paragraph describing transactions between "Principals of the General Partners" (officers of the investment group) and "General Partners" (investors) says,

> Each of the members of [the investment group], as officers, directors and shareholders of Resources, have entered into a Shareholder Agreement which provides for, among other things . . . certain rights of first refusal for Resources and the other shareholders if one shareholder desires to dispose of his stock in Resources. . . .

Notice that in addition to including an agreement error ("Each of the members . . . have entered"), the passage employs the masculine pronoun, *his*, implying all shareholders are male. The assumption is unwarranted. Women as well as men invest in limited partnerships.

I return to an earlier point to justify this chapter's attention to inclusive language. Some writers and readers see the substitution of neutral labels and gender-free pronouns as a political statement. Readers who resist the current trend toward inclusive language may be distracted by obvious substitutions. The goal of the writer, therefore, must be to make the changes so graceful, so natural, that the reader is unaware the issue has arisen. The guidelines in this chapter should help.

GUIDELINES

Among the strategies that will help a writer avoid thinking in gender-related stereotypes, I will mention only three of the most obvious.

25. Never use *man* or *mankind* to refer to all of humanity.

No matter what our schoolteachers told us, *man* excludes one half of the human population. Our sensitivity to this exclusion has increased in the past twenty years. Even *mankind*, clearly intended to include both sexes, will be read by some as exclusive. Good writers, alert to audience, will avoid any construction that offends or excludes readers. The most concise justification for using inclusive terms that I know is in a footnote in Peter Farb's book *Humankind* (Houghton Mifflin, 1978). Farb explains that throughout his book he has avoided using *man* to refer to our species. He has preferred such terms as *humankind, human beings,* and *people.* Farb adds,

> I have also avoided the grammatical use of masculine pronouns (unless, of course, the male sex is specifically referred to), sex-linked nouns (such as "poetess"), and sex-role stereotypes (such as the assumption that "secretary" is of the female gender). To some readers, my concern may appear exaggerated—but it is valid. This book attempts to get at our essential humanity. It cannot do so if my perspective is distorted and sustained by a male-oriented vocabulary.
>
> [Humankind, p. 3]

26. Use labels that do not suggest the sex of the person referred to.

IN PLACE OF	USE
postman	*letter carrier*
stewardess	*flight attendant*
waitress	*server, food server*
coed	*student*
lady policeman	*police officer*
male nurse	*nurse*
career woman	*professional*
businessman	*business executive, manager*
chairman, chairwoman	*chair, chairperson*

Finding labels that do not sound cumbersome is not always easy. Some labels have emerged slowly as a result of experimentation. A decade ago the most common strategy for replacing words with *man* in them was substituting *person: chairperson, wait person, police person.* In most contexts we now have well accepted labels that are not direct substitutions.

27. Treat men and women equally.

Do not feel you are flattering women by referring to them delicately as *ladies*. In some situations it may be appropriate to refer to *ladies and gentlemen*, but the term that corresponds to *men* is *women*. Even worse, of course, would be to refer to office workers in clerical positions as *the girls in the office*. If the office personnel where you work are all women, it is appropriate in many instances to refer to them using feminine pronouns. But they are women, not girls.

Even in an occupation where representation of the sexes is not equal, it is wrong to assume that all members of the occupation are of one sex.

Example: *The new incentive program encourages every fireman to keep himself fit.*

Correction: *The new incentive program encourages fire fighters to keep themselves fit.*

Example: *The leading salesmen are rewarded with a weekend at an attractive resort. Their wives and children are invited.*

Correction: *The leading sales representatives are rewarded with a weekend at an attractive resort. Their families are invited.*

In the course of writing about customers, public personalities, or people in the news, treat them with equal respect.

Example: *Several Texas mayors attended the ceremonies: Bolen from Fort Worth, Cisneros from San Antonio, and Annette Strauss from Dallas.*

Correction: *Several Texas mayors attended the ceremonies: Bolen from Fort Worth, Cisneros from San Antonio, and Strauss from Dallas.*

Alternate Correction: *Several Texas mayors attended the ceremonies: Bob Bolen from Fort Worth, Henry Cisneros from San Antonio, and Annette Strauss from Dallas.*

Example: *At the board meeting yesterday, our president, Mrs. Althea Ryan, asked treasurer Richard Flandermeyer to prepare a report on the year's expenses. Mrs. Ryan requested that Flandermeyer have the figures by the next meeting.*

Correction: *At the board meeting yesterday, president Althea Ryan asked treasurer Richard Flandermeyer to prepare a report on the year's expenses. Ryan requested that Flandermeyer have the figures by the next meeting.*

28. Avoid masculine pronouns used to include both sexes.

The second stage in overcoming sexist language is to command the grammar, specifically the pronouns with gender, in such a way as to avoid excluding one sex or the other. Here again, the recent history of good usage helps us discover strategies that avoid sexual exclusiveness without introducing awkwardness. Combing your text for uses of *he*, *him*, or *his* used generically and replacing the single pronouns with alternatives, *s/he, him or her, his/her*, avoids the problem of exclusiveness, but it makes the prose clumsy. A good writer will find more graceful ways of editing sexist language. No single strategy will work in every case. Knowing which of the several options is appro-

priate depends on having a good ear and a sure sense of
the intent of the passage.

28a.   Drop the pronoun if possible.

Example: *On trips for the company each representative
should keep a record of his expenses as well as an
envelope of receipts.*

Correction: *On trips for the company each representative
should keep a record of expenses as well as an envelope of receipts.*

Example: *Every letter writer has his own way of opening his
first paragraph.*

Correction: *Every letter writer has a unique way of opening
the first paragraph.*

28b.   Use first or second person or substitute the plural.

The goal here is to use pronouns without separate masculine and feminine forms. Both the first person, *I* or *we,*
and the second person, *you,* can refer to either male or
female. The plural *they* also avoids implying a sex.

Example: *Thus the reader of this guide is warned that he
must become a user, that he must practice what he
learns or he will soon forget it.*

Correction: *Thus as the reader of this guide you are warned
that you must become a user, that you must practice
what you learn or you will soon forget it.*

Alternate correction: *Thus readers of this guide are warned
that they must become users, that they must practice
what they learn or they will soon forget it.*

Example: *When the student or employee logs on to the computer he must enter his identification number to insure proper billing for the computer time.*

Correction: *When you log on to the computer enter your identification number to insure proper billing for the computer time.*

Example: *In this organization each member has his own assignment and reports his own achievements to the front office.*

Correction: *In this organization we all have our own assignments and report our own achievements to the front office.*

In using this strategy for avoiding pronouns with masculine or feminine gender, it is important to keep in mind guideline 5b. If you use plural pronouns or shift to first or second person, you must be careful to keep the person and number consistent throughout the passage.

28c. Use plural personal pronouns with singular indefinite pronouns.

Example: *For this assignment everyone is expected to gather his own background figures.*

Correction: *For this assignment everyone is expected to gather their own background figures.*

Alternate correction: *For this assignment you are expected to gather your own background figures.*

The plural pronoun in the first correction violates Guideline 8a., that indefinite pronouns are usually singular. Using *their* introduces an agreement error. Some writers prefer the grammatically flawed sentence to using *his* as a generic pronoun. But as the alternate correction demonstrates, other solutions are available. Whether the alternate correction is preferable depends on the context of the sentence.

28d.   Use the passive voice or some other impersonal construction.

Example: *Each client has his own file, which he keeps separate from the general files.*

Correction: *Individual client files are kept separate from the general files.*

Alternate correction: *There are individual files which each client keeps separate from the general files.*

The danger in this strategy for avoiding pronouns with gender is that it introduces awkwardness of a different sort. The writer should experiment with various ways of eliminating sex-referenced pronouns. A better solution might be found that keeps the sentence in active form: *Each client has a separate file, which the client keeps separate from the general files.* This correction repeats *the client* and therefore might be rejected as cumbersome.

No single strategy for eliminating pronouns with gender can be regarded as appropriate for all situations. It may turn out that occasionally a writer will use *he or she* as the most graceful expression of an idea. So long as the phrase is used only occasionally and does not appear to be a thoughtless, automatic substitution, a writer can feel confident in using the phrase. However, avoid *s/he* altogether.

29.   Alternate male and female examples.

A writer preparing a report on intercollegiate athletics might deal with living conditions on the college campus, with pressure to keep academic achievement high, perhaps with recruiting strategies. The writer would strive for the sparkle of concrete examples, specific illustrations. In doing so the writer would inevitably refer to real people, particular athletes and college personnel. To avoid bias in the report, the writer should mix the examples to include female athletes as well as male athletes.

In a piece on insurance claims, the writer should illustrate with claimants of both sexes rather than use generic masculine pronouns. The writer should cite domestic situations that avoid traditional or stereotyped roles.

In this excerpt from an article on gifted children, the writer provides several examples, all using generic masculine pronouns:

> Whereas the average child in school tends to learn what he is taught in the order he is taught it, the gifted child tends to see resonances between ideas and concepts that go far beyond the immediate learning task. Within Bloom's taxonomy, he may leap from knowledge to synthesis in a given area, simply because he has already gone through all the intermediary steps on his own. He may devise his own problem-solving approach, thereby blocking out whatever "conflicting" rules he is being taught. He may project a given topic onto a related area about which he already has strong feelings, thus allowing his personal "viewpoint" to "interfere" with what he is supposed to learn.

The writer has used three examples to illustrate how differently a gifted child learns. All three examples are presented as gifted boys. The writer could as easily have alternated between boys and girls:

> Within Bloom's taxonomy, a gifted boy may leap from knowledge to synthesis. . . . A bright girl may devise her own problem-solving approach. . . .

The writer would have to be adroit to avoid suggesting that children of one sex are more likely to be gifted, children of the other sex more likely to be average. Notice the undesirable implications of alternating the gender of pronouns carelessly:

> Whereas the average child in school tends to learn what he is taught in the order he is taught it, the gifted child tends to see resonances in her learning, linking ideas and concepts that go beyond the immediate task.

Avoiding sexist language is not easy. No one said it was.

30.   For business letters use neutral forms of address.

The women's movement has provided a form of address for women that avoids distinguishing between married and unmarried women. *Ms.* is convenient for written communications. Not a dodge to be used when the writer is unsure of the woman's marital status, Ms. is a positive gesture of equal treatment, demonstrating that in most situations—in business transactions, certainly—marital status is irrelevant.

The perplexing issue in beginning a letter is what form to use if you don't know the sex of the person or persons you are addressing. In a salutation to the editorial board of a magazine it would be a tactical error to begin, *Gentlemen.* It would be equally insensitive to address the board of directors of any organization, *Dear Sirs.* The most diplomatic strategies for addressing groups of either sex or of both sexes are those that avoid any suggestion of gender.

30a. If you don't know the name, use the generic title.

Most titles lend themselves to such use: Dear Editor, Dear Commissioner, Dear Programming Superviser, Dear Committee Chair.

Example: *Director of Marketing*
            California Pioneer Insurance Company
            1250 Eighth Avenue
            San Diego, California 92101

            Dear Marketing Director:

30b.   If you know the name but are unsure of the sex, use the full name.

Some writers prefer this form of address even when the first name appears to suggest the sex of the person addressed. Many given names are used for both sexes.

Example: *Morgan Rogers, Director of Admissions*
            Oklahoma State University
            Stillwater, Oklahoma

            Dear Morgan Rogers:

30c.   Omit the line of salutation.

Particularly when letters are addressed to companies or to groups with a corporate identity, it is perfectly good form to eliminate such awkward salutations as *Dear Product Division* or *Dear Litton Microwave Cooking Products.*

Example: *Reference Software International*
            330 Townsend Street
            San Francisco, CA 94107

            My review of your Grammatik IV User's Guide reveals that . . .

Since the address does not indicate who will receive the letter, the writer risks nothing by not identifying a person or a title. A letter addressed to the company will hardly pass for a personal note. To make up a title is no better than using none.

Selecting the right form of salutation comes under the heading of good manners. It is less at the heart of inclusive writing than guidelines 1 through 5. Yet the salutation line is often the first part of a letter the reader pays attention to. The success of a letter, like the success of all writing, depends on including all members of your audience.

What finally matters in editing to eliminate sexist bias is attention to the issue. Rather than develop a single or favorite strategy, it is best to consider a range of options. Because every situation is different, a writer must remain alert. No style guide can ask more.

EXERCISES

Revising to eliminate sexist language is seldom a matter of changing a word here and there, using gender-free pronouns to replace *he*. Often a writer must recast whole sentences or find alternative examples to illustrate a point. The exercises for this chapter, therefore, are not identified with specific guidelines. Nearly all the passages require applying several guidelines at once.

Refer to guidelines 25–30.

1. The following passage is from the pamphlet on selling used in Chapter Four to illustrate sexist language and sexist generalizations. Can it be rewritten to eliminate the writer's exclusive language? As you revise the passage, you may want to make other improvements in style and mechanics.

Just as the tremendous power of steam is the result of bringing water and heat together, a salesman can become most
powerful when he combines salesmanship and conviction. For
an insurance agent a burning conviction that his product is the
best property in the world is a great source of power. But, conviction by itself isn't enough! There are many men in this business, such as actuaries, investment officers, and others, who
are thoroughly convinced that insurance is indeed a financial
miracle—they have the conviction but they don't sell it.

On the other hand, it is possible to attain a certain degree
of skill in salesmanship without a belief in your product or a
conviction in the benefits you offer your prospects. However,
this type of salesmanship has never produced a great salesman nor lasting benefits to the prospect, the company, or
the salesman.

It is only when you combine skill as a salesman with a
deep-seated belief in the benefits of your service that you
have the unbeatable combination. This is not only true for
great insurance salesmen, but the greatest men of history
were men with the conviction that their cause was right and
with the ability to persuade men to follow them. Such men as
Paul, Caesar, Napoleon, Washington, and Churchill are
examples of the power created by combining salesmanship
and conviction.

2. Revise the following paragraph from the technical
writer's style manual quoted in Chapter Four.

First, and most important, the writer must make a conscious
effort to adapt to the reader. In making this effort he must
play a dual role: the writer (the expert, the giver of information) and the reader (the nonexpert, the seeker of information). The writer's job is to perform well in both roles. When
he does, that which is clear to him will be made clear to his
reader. The reader, then, must always be present during the

writing process, looking over the writer's shoulder so to speak, always questioning, never satisfied.

[General Dynamic Guide to Achieving Style, p. 5]

3. The following paragraph is modified slightly from an article in a collection of readings on education. Revise it to remove the sexist language.

From the biological point of view, under the microscope, man is similar to other animals. Their metabolisms are the same, but he doesn't behave like the others. He is the only species that discovered how to adapt his surroundings to himself, not himself to his surroundings. Man was probably born in the very hot and humid tropical climate of Africa. He can recreate that climate in the middle of Greenland, in a igloo; with a seal oil flame that he causes to burn, he obtains a hot and humid atmosphere. Man is the only animal who does not submit to his environment but is its coauthor. He has done even better; to the two sources of genes and environment, he has added a third source: the collective indestructible memory based on writing.

4. In the next paragraphs, about writing research (from a third edition, dated 1977), the authors have acknowledged the need to include both sexes by using *he* or *she*. Apparently their commitment to fair treatment has not been strong enough to produce a complete revision. Correct the paragraph to eliminate its bias.

In setting out the difficulties of method and theory in the "new disciplines," one runs the risk of giving the casual reader the impression of partisan opposition. That is a false impression. The historian, of all people, recognizes the right of any student to use the materials of the past as he or she sees fit. The historian not only knows, but points out that sociology, psychology, anthropology, demography are integral parts of history, that they came into being out of the womb of history. The historian, too, is and has been eager to count things, men, distances whenever he could, the knowledge of magnitudes being essential to many narratives. Finally, the historian is ready to make use of any other relevant data brought him by experts using special methods— the chemist who tests a piece of paper with reagents or the physicist who dates a relic by measuring the radiation of its components.

It follows that the historian does not reject out of hand studies in historical sociology or psychological analysis. Only, he insists that for his purposes they must meet the standards of evidence, cogency, and probability that he applies to all his materials without exception. To be sure, he takes the chemist's and the physicist's results for granted, because the consensus about methods in each science is a notorious fact. He cannot similarly accept the psycho- and quanto-historian's results, first because such a consensus on methods is lacking, and also because students who use them are dealing with the historian's own materials, about which he must be allowed to know something.

5. The following sentences are flawed in ways that illustrate the most common abuses of the generic masculine pronoun. Revise them to make them inclusive.

a. A good carpenter knows his tools and keeps them clean, sharp, and ready for use.

b. Each passenger is responsible for his own luggage. He should have each bag or package tagged with his name and address.

c. Anyone who wants his paper returned should include a self-addressed, stamped envelope.

d. A good letter writer crafts the opening of a letter carefully, aware that a good impression begins with the first sentence. He doesn't spin his wheels.

He never starts with a word that ends in "ing":

Referring . . .

Replying . . .

He never starts with a phrase that ends with the preposition "to":

With reference to . . .

In answer to . . .

Pursuant to . . .

He never starts with a redundant expression:

I am writing . . .

For your information . . .

This is to inform you . . .

The purpose of this letter is . . .

We have received your letter . . .

Enclosed please find . . .

Attached herewith . . .

[Adapted from a textbook on technical writing]

e. The artist's job in the beginning is not unlike the job of a writer. He or she must first reach out for raw material. He or she must spend much time making contact with actual objects. He or she must learn to see—to see correctly—using as many of the five senses as can reach through the eye at one time. [Adapted from The Natural Way to Draw, p. 5]

Chapter Five

On Writing at the Computer

Of the many ways computers have changed our writing, two have a bearing on matters considered in this book. The first is how we manage repetitive letters, the routine correspondence that many companies or institutions send their customers or clients dealing with the same or similar situations again and again. Most companies store such letters electronically. The second is whether and how writers rely on computers to perform simple editing. A wide range of software is available to analyze our writing and to make suggestions about spelling, grammar, and style. I will deal with these technological innovations simply and briefly.

REPETITIVE LETTERS

The challenge in writing repetitive letters is to disguise what they are. Chapter One argues that even business letters can be personal. To be personal a letter has to suggest that the writer has a specific reader in mind and that the writer is aware of every circumstance surrounding the transaction. Conveying such personal concern is fairly easy when the writer is dealing with a fresh case each time and studies the circumstances before writing the letter. But what does the writer do who must write the same letter to fifteen clients a day, changing only the policy numbers or interest rates or terms of payment according to the particular client?

To make a letter personal, a writer has to imagine the letter will go to a particular person, as of course it will.

However often the letter is sent, one person receives it every time. A thoughtful writer refers to the person addressed as *you* and to herself or himself as *I* or *me*. The writer also avoids those conventional phrases that make letters sound institutional. Consider the following form letter, used when one bank writes another to inform the second bank that a certificate of deposit is being used as collateral on a loan. The information in brackets would vary from letter to letter.

[Date]

[Institution and address]

Re: Certificate of Deposit
[number]
[Name]

Gentlemen:

This letter is to inform you we have accepted the above captioned account as security for a loan to [name].

We would appreciate you signing the acknowledgment below, keeping one copy for your files and returning one copy to us for our files.

If you have any questions, please contact the undersigned.

Very truly yours,

[R. C. Turner]
Vice President

Acknowledgment:

_____
[Institution]

Notice how simply the writer could make this letter sound more personal.

[Date]

[Institution and address]

Re: Certificate of Deposit
[number]
[Name]

We have accepted certificate of deposit # [account number] as security for a loan to [name].

You can help us by signing the acknowledgment below, keeping one copy for your files, and returning one copy to us.

If you have any questions, please contact me.

Very truly yours,

[R. C. Turner]
Vice President

Acknowledgment:

_____

[Institution]

In editing the letter I have removed the heading *Gentlemen* because it is sexist. I have omitted *you* before *signing* to eliminate the need for a possessive before a **gerund**—a grammatical nicety that can be avoided. I have also trimmed away the round-about opening, *This letter is to inform you.* The letter in its edited form is streamlined. More important, the letter sounds as if it were written from one person to another.

Notice, all the information that varies from one letter to

another—date, address, and the like—can still be filled in on a form letter stored in a computer.

One more example will serve to establish that letters with a personal flavor are no more difficult to compose and process than letters marred by a distant, even hostile tone. In this example I have provided the information, in brackets, that would vary from letter to letter.

[January 21, 1991]

[Richard Labor
Labor Loan Company
Campobella, SC 29322]
RE: [1984 Toyota P/U David Anders]

To Whom It May Concern:

This is your authority to act as our agent in repossession of [a 1984 Toyota P/U, JT4RN67SXFR034276] from [David Anders, work phone 926-0434]. Customer has an address of [2825 Wood Dr., Fort Worth, Texas 76018].

We agree to indemnify and to save you harmless from and against any and all claims, damages, losses and actions resulting from or arising out of your efforts to repossess the above account, except, such as may be caused by or arise out of negligency or unauthorized acts of your firm, its officers or employees.

Please do not under any circumstances assign this case to an attorney or any other firm without authorization in writing from the undersigned.

Attached are copies of title and Motor Vehicle Contract.

Sincerely,

Pat Wanley
Assistant Vice President

The bank sending this letter may have no reason to establish personal relations with the collection agencies it uses. But even business relations can be more pleasant if the letters sound like ordinary talk produced by real people. Someone, after all, will sign the letter. It might sound like this:

[January 21, 1991]

[Richard Labor
Labor Loan Company
Campobella, SC 29322]
RE: [1984 Toyota P/U David Anders]

Dear [Richard Labor]:

    You are authorized as our agent to repossess [a 1984 Toyota P/U, JT4RN67SXFR034276] from [David Anders, work phone 926-0434]. The address of [David Anders] is [2825 Wood Dr., Fort Worth, Texas 76018].

    We agree to indemnify and to save you harmless from and against any and all claims, damages, losses and actions resulting from or arising out of your efforts to repossess the above account, except, such as may be caused by or arise out of negligency or unauthorized acts of your firm, its officers or employees.

    Please do not assign this case to an attorney or any other firm without authorization from me.

    We have attached copies of the title and the Motor Vehicle Contract.

Sincerely,

Pat Wanley
Assistant Vice President

The middle paragraph of this letter, probably written by an attorney, bears the stamp of legal writing, most conspicuously the repeated nouns and verbs intended to cover all possibilities. I have left the paragraph alone, temporarily, because I anticipate the legal department will tell me I can't change it for reasons of liability. The assistant vice president may prefer an attorney's advice to that of a writing coach. The truth is, the middle paragraph can be streamlined some without losing its legal force:

> We agree to indemnify you against any claims, damages, losses and actions that result from your efforts to repossess the property unless they arise out of your negligence or unauthorized acts of you or your employees.

How important it is to put this paragraph in plain English depends on the company that uses it. Some may prefer the more official sound of the original. Chances are, the loan company will not read it carefully in any case. A company that takes pride in its correspondence, however, would want to compose and edit stored letters thoughtfully to reflect its personal style.

EDITING SOFTWARE

Anyone who uses a computer program to check spelling is aware that the spelling check serves two important functions. The first is to catch typographical errors resulting from carelessness. The second is to help the writer spell difficult words. The spelling checker will not catch the third kind of misspelling, covered under guideline 13, errors resulting from the wrong choice of two acceptable words. This classification of spelling errors can be applied to the analysis of style and grammar provided by the most common style checkers.

The pace of developments in editing software is so rapid that a description of the editing capabilities of a specific program would be out of date before it could be published. I intend, therefore, to base my advice in this section on a broad consideration of the kinds of decisions an editing program makes.

The simplest kind of information a computer analysis provides is counting sentences, words, and syllables. At least three tests of readability are based on such information; the Flesch Index of readability, Gunning's Fog Index, and the Flesch-Kincaid Index use either an arbitrary scale or a hypothetical school grade level to indicate whether the writing is easy or difficult to read. The scores or grade levels are derived from the number of sentences per paragraph, the number of words per sentence, and the number of syllables per word. Such information is useful to a writer so long as the writer recognizes the scales are arbitrary and the "reading levels" have nothing to do with effective style and little to do with readability.

The stylistic advice a computer can provide is based on guidelines similar to those in this book. The style checker may look for signals of passive voice, frequent use of forms of *be*, and the expletives *there* and *it* used with forms of *be*. A writer can use help identifying such potentially ineffective constructions. One virtue of the computer is that it never gets careless or lazy; it never misses a construction it is programmed to catch. On the other hand, the software cannot interpret language, cannot distinguish between careless repetition and deliberate effects, cannot at present make judgments based on the syntax of a sentence.

A few examples illustrate the limitations of computer analysis. This sentence from a legal brief provides confusing signals to the computer.

> *The major legal issue presented by Plaintiffs' Motion for Partial Summary Judgment is whether adopted*

> children are entitled to take any of the proceeds of the
> Testamentary Trust created by the will of W.W.
> Fellows.

Grammatik IV identifies two passive constructions in the sentence and warns the writer to reconsider them. The first construction, *is . . . adopted*, turns out not to be a passive; the computer fails to recognize that a subordinate clause begins with *whether*. The second passive construction, *are entitled*, should be flagged. Though not out of place in this context, the verb is passive. A good writer wants to be alerted to passive constructions so as to avoid overusing them. The style checker also notices that *W. W.* is a repetition and asks the writer if the doubled word should be deleted. Finally, because the sentence contains 36 words, the style checker suggests revising.

Here are some illustrations using the Lewis Thomas essay, "On Warts."

> It seems to me hardly enough for the mind to say,
> simply, get off, eliminate yourselves, without providing
> something in the way of specifications as to how to go
> about it.

The computer notices *to* followed by *how* and is confused. It accepts *to* followed by a verb form as an **infinitive**, and it allows *to* as a preposition followed by a noun. The computer suspects that the proper form before *how* is either *too* or *two*. Remember the computer can't really read.

> If my unconscious can figure out how to manipulate the
> mechanisms needed for getting around that virus . . . .

Here the computer recognizes *unconscious* as an adjective, but not a noun, and points out that an adjective is seldom followed by a verb. No dictionary can include every use of every word. The programmers rely on the writer to take charge when an unorthodox construction triggers a warning.

The program used to analyze these sentences also warns against split infinitives and cautions a writer not to end a sentence with a preposition. I suspect the style checker retains these proscriptions because violations are easy to spot. And in fairness, a writer should discard such advice only for legitimate reasons. Good writers are aware that some readers are distracted by split infinitives and sentences that end in prepositions. Good writers use these constructions only if they will achieve a desirable effect.

Style checkers can help us deal with carelessness, ignorance, and false choices. A writer who slips carelessly into a style dominated by forms of *be* needs to be alerted that the style is indirect. A writer who has not read this book or others like it may need to be told that *there* and *it*, used as expletives, erode the force of otherwise fluent prose. But the writer needs to recognize that no computerized analysis can take the place of careful reading, conscious decisions, and attention to detail. Ultimately, the writer is responsible for all choices. My advice is, don't pass up useful help wherever you can find it, but don't be tyrannized by an editor that can't read.

CONCLUSION

My advice about computer spelling checkers and style checkers applies to this book as well. Just as a style checker cannot read your text, a book on editing cannot anticipate every situation in which you write. It can't make allowances for stylistic maneuvers, deliberate repetitions, or intentional strategies that violate the guidelines. Good writers sometimes intentionally violate the guidelines. Nor can a guide of this size cover all the principles all writers think are important. The need for simplicity and directness outweighs the demand for comprehensive coverage.

The most you can expect of this book is that it covers the most important matters, the clumsy phrases most likely to interfere with crisp writing. I have tried to provide a limited set of guidelines, stated directly, illustrated simply. I have insisted from the beginning they are not rules. When the guidelines appear to help your writing, observe them; they should give you confidence. When the guidelines seem to be leading you to a style you don't like, ignore them.

The person responsible for the writing you produce is you.

Corrections for the Exercises

CHAPTER ONE: GUIDELINES FOR COMPOSING

This section provides my solutions to the composing and editing problems the exercises present. They are not "right" answers. For each sentence I have tried to make my editing decisions clear. You may not agree with me. So long as you consider carefully why the revision is suggested, you should feel confident about rejecting my solution.

1. Find the true subject and correct verb.

1. Advanced courses should be designed specifically to utilize and reinforce competencies (knowledge and skills) acquired in the completion of preliminary coursework.

    Correction:

    Instructors should design advanced courses to use and reinforce the knowledge and skills taught in preliminary courses.

    Explanation:

    Eliminating the passive construction, *should be designed*, is desirable on stylistic grounds. The writer might prefer to keep the passive, however, if the writer is not sure individual instructors design their own courses. *Use* is a simpler word that means the same thing as *utilize* (see guideline 7a). If *competencies* means *knowledge and skills*, as the parenthetical addition suggests, the sentence can be shortened by avoiding *competencies*. Except in technical contexts, it is best not to use a word that must be explained. Notice that the simple word *taught* replaces two less familiar words, *acquired* and *completion*.

2. This utilization may be achieved through the coordinated use of computers, research projects, and written assignments in the courses.

Correction:

   Students can be required to use their knowledge and skills in coordinated computer exercises, research projects, and written assignments.

Explanation:

   In correcting this sentence I have assumed that sentence 2 is an elaboration of sentence 1. If the sentences were not together in the exercise, I would have devised some other correction. The phrase *this utilization* implies a context of some sort, a context I would use in correcting the sentence. Notice that the noun *use* has been changed to a verb with the same form. It replaces the abstract *utilization*. *Coordinated* is ambiguous in the original sentence. We can't be sure whether it modifies only *use of computers* or whether it modifies the series of three strategies. I have preserved this ambiguity, hoping the context would clarify the meaning. *In the course* adds nothing to the sentence.

3. If the purchase is approved, final negotiations are completed, the purchase agreement is finalized, all remaining escrow contingencies are removed, and the title is transferred.

Correction:

   If your purchase is approved, we will complete final negotiations, including the purchase agreement, remove remaining escrow contingencies, and transfer your title.

Explanation:

   Because I couldn't come up with a better synonym for *finalize* than *complete*, I included the purchase agreement among the items to be completed. The context might argue against this simplification. The principal improvement in the corrected form is removing the passive constructions. To make this improvement I have had to assume the sentence is directed to a buyer whom the writer will help.

4. For its larger mission to be possible, it will be necessary for additional resources to be found and allocated to the college.

Correction:

The college needs additional resources to pursue its mission.

Explanation:

Because of the passive constructions I can't be sure who will find and allocate resources to the college. In simplifying the sentence I have removed the sense that some anonymous angel will appear out of the mist. The writer might not be pleased to see the stark message that the sentence conveys.

5. The decision about the choice of the right course of action was made by the night nurse, acting entirely on her own.

Correction:

The night nurse decided what to do entirely on her own.

Alternate correction:

The night nurse, alone, decided what to do.

Explanation:

The ambiguity of the modifier *entirely on her own* is not solved by the first correction. We don't know whether the nurse decided on her own to act or whether she decided to act on her own. Probably both are intended. The alternate correction assumes that *on her own* is meant to modify *decided* even though in the original sentence the phrase modifies *acting*.

6. Data were collected concerning high school students

interest in engineering as well as the quality and types of applicants. In addition, current and projected enrollment and job demand information for engineering students were analyzed. Other programs were examined to determine the need for resources, including faculty, equipment, additional library holdings, facilities needs, etc. Questions concerning the impact of such a program on other programs, including residential living needs, were explored. Finally, estimated costs were gathered based on the experience of other universities.

Correction:

We collected data on high school students' interest in engineering and on the quality and types of applicants. We analyzed current and projected enrollment and the job demand for engineering students. We examined other programs to determine the need for resources, including faculty, equipment, library holdings, facilities, and the like. We explored the impact of such a program on other programs, including residential living. Finally we based an estimate of the costs on the experience of other universities.

Explanation:

The information in this paragraph remains abstract. The passage is more direct, however, and sounds less bureaucratic in the active voice. I have replaced *etc.* with *and the like*. Strictly used, *etc.* refers to a list already established or known to the reader. It should not be used to refer to unspecified additions to a list.

7. Employees are required by company policy to report additional income earned by outside consulting.

Correction:

Company policy requires that employees report additional income they earn by outside consulting.

Explanation:

This sentence is not dramatically improved by the revision. The context might make the original sentence preferable. Converting from passive to active voice shifts the emphasis from employees to company policy.

8. Elimination of unneeded paper and unutilized forms can be achieved by judicious use of the paper shredder.

    Correction:

    Use the shredder to get rid of waste paper and unused forms.

    Explanation:

    The revision coverts an abstract statement to a simple directive.

9. Reading stations are provided for examination of newly received materials prior to check-out.

    Correction:

    We provide reading stations where you can examine new materials before checking them out.

    Explanation:

    The first correction is to convert passive to active voice. Changing *newly received* to *new* and *prior to* to *before* improves the readability of the sentence.

10. This is an exaggeration on your part of the significance of the role of the new equipment.

    Correction:

    You exaggerate the significance of the new equipment.

    Explanation:

    Converting the abstract nominalization is the simple part of this correction. The harder decision is whether the person addressed exaggerates the significance of the new equipment or the role of the new equipment. Without correction, the sentence ends in four prepositional phrases.

11. Your contribution to our agency is appreciated.

    Correction:

    We appreciate your contribution to the agency.

Alternate correction:

The agency appreciates your contribution.

Explanation:

The two corrections convey slightly different emphasis. Which is preferable would depend on the contribu-
tor's relations with the agency.

12. Make an estimate of the amount of time spent by you
before submitting your report.

Correction:

Estimate the time you spent before you submitted
your report.

Alternate correction:

Estimate the time you spent before you submit your
report.

Explanation:

The difference in these two corrections reflects the
ambiguity of the example sentence. To correct the sentence we must decide whether the person is to estimate
time spent before reporting or whether the person is
expected to estimate before submitting the report.

13. If the cost is known, make an entry of the amount in
the first column.

Correction:

If you know the cost, enter the amount in the first
column.

Explanation:

As an abstract nominalization, *entry* is a minor
offender. And yet *enter* is more direct than *make an
entry*.

14. Analysis of the data is done by computer.

Correction:

A computer analyzes our data.

Alternate correction:

We use a computer to analyze data.

Explanation:

Which of these corrections you prefer will depend in part on your attitude toward computers.

15. Recent expansion of the building has contributed to the easing of congestion in the corridors.

    Correction:

    Recent expansion of the building has eased congestion in the corridors.

    Alternate correction:

    We have eased congestion in the corridors by expanding the building.

    Second alternate correction:

    The corridors are less congested since we expanded the building.

    Explanation:

    Even a fairly simple sentence can often be improved in a variety of ways. The writer would have to decide which of these corrections was best.

16. A survey of students was conducted to arrive at an estimate of the level of student use at peak hours.

    Correction:

    We surveyed students to estimate student use at peak hours.

    Alternate correction:

    We surveyed students to estimate the level of student use at peak hours.

    Explanation:

    Some writers might contend that estimating student use is different from estimating the level of student use. Those who do would prefer the alternate correction.

2. Take noun phrases apart.

1. The significance of observation to the practice of qual-

ity nursing care has been well documented in the literature. However, documentation of the role of observation in the development and subsequent implementation of research activities has been limited.

Correction:

The significance of observation to the practice of nursing has been well documented. The role of observation in research activities, however, has been less well documented.

Explanation:

It is not possible to eliminate all prepositional phrases from abstract statements such as this one. Notice, however, that chains of prepositional phrases suggest some trimming is possible. Here a number of abstract nominalizations clog the prose.

2. The library has a book of familiar quotations of famous authors.

Correction:

The library has a book containing familiar quotations of famous authors.

Explanation:

The corrected sentence has the same number of words as the original sentence. Changing one preposition to a verb form improves the rhythm of the sentence by shortening the string of prepositional phrases.

3. The construction of a new wing of 9,000 sq. ft. on the east end of the building will contribute to the relief of congestion.

Correction:

Adding a wing of 9,000 sq. ft. on the east end of the building will help to relieve congestion.

Alternate correction:

We can relieve some congestion by adding a wing of 9,000 sq. ft. on the east end of the building.

Explanation:

We can't be sure the context will permit the writer to provide a grammatical subject, *we*. But even with the subject unstated, we tighten the sentence by replacing the abstract nominalization *construction* with the verb form *adding*. The chain of prepositional phrases, *of a new wing of 9,000 sq. ft. on the east end of the building*, is cumbersome. Converting the string to *a 9,000 sq. ft. wing on the building's east end* would not improve the sentence.

4. It is impossible to make an accurate estimate of the time of arrival of every vehicle in our fleet.

Correction:

We cannot accurately estimate the arrival time of every vehicle in our fleet.

Explanation:

Changing *make an estimate* to *estimate* is a correction suggested by guideline 7c. *Arrival time* is preferable to *time of arrival* only because the change shortens the chain of prepositional phrases by one.

5. Every one of the solutions to this problem has at least one flaw.

Correction:

Every solution to this problem has at least one flaw.

Explanation:

A useful rule of thumb to store away: wherever you encounter *each of* or *every one of*, followed by a plural, the phrase can be simplified by writing *each* or *every*, followed by the singular. This rule, like most rules of thumb, has many exceptions.

6. The university's placement of a student into an agency for the purpose of field education brings a number of reciprocal responsibilities into action.

Correction:

By placing a student in an agency for field

education, the university triggers a number of reciprocal responsibilities.

Alternate correction:

By placing a student in an agency for field education, the university activates a number of reciprocal responsibilities.

Explanation:

By introducing the metaphorical *trigger*, I have made this sentence less formal than it was. The alternate correction avoids this liberty.

7. Design Inc. is a well respected Dallas-based graphics business consulting firm.

Correction:

Design Inc. is a well respected graphics consulting firm in Dallas.

Explanation:

The noun phrase in the original sentence is difficult to unpack. Whether Design Inc. is a graphics firm doing business consulting or a consulting firm for the graphics business is not clear. The writer presumably knows the business well and regards the sentence as clear. But precisely because the sentence is confusing to anyone but the writer, it needs work.

8. We have included our business client reference list and a current CDS annual report. We normally prepare a more comprehensive proposal or full-scale fund raising action plan but, due to your quick-reaction timing requirements, we have submitted this short term memo at your request. We would like the opportunity to meet with you to discuss the project in more detail and to respond with a more formalized document regarding our approach to your needs.

Correction:

We include a list of client references and a current CDS annual report. We normally prepare a more comprehensive proposal or a plan for fund raising, but to meet your timing needs we have prepared this brief memo. We would like to meet with you to discuss the project in more detail and to present a more formal document detailing our approach to your needs.

Explanation:

The offending phrases in this paragraph are the tightly packed noun phrases, *full scale fund raising action plan* and *quick-reaction timing requirements*. The paragraph sounds as if it was written in a hurry. Also troublesome is the phrase *would like the opportunity to meet*. The passage can be trimmed without loss of content. The number of words has been reduced from 75 to 65. The improvement is not that the rewritten version is shorter, but that it is less strained.

3.   Choose the most direct statement.

1. By acquiring oil and gas properties only where wells have been in production for some time it is possible for our investors to obtain the benefits of owning valuable natural resources—oil and gas—without exposure to the significant risks of drilling.

    Correction:

    Because we acquire oil and gas properties only where wells have been in production for some time, our investors can obtain the benefits of owning valuable natural resorces—oil and gas—without the risks of drilling.

    Alternate correction:

    Because we acquire oil and gas properties only where wells have been in production for some time, we can offer our investors the benefits of owning valuable natural resorces—oil and gas—without the risks of drilling.

    Explanation:

    The grammatical subject of this sentence is

displaced by the expletive *it*. The introductory phrase is
therefore a dangling modifier (covered in guideline 9).
The logical subject is *investors*, buried in an infinitive
phrase. Changing the introductory phrase to a subordinate clause eliminates the dangling modifier. The
sense of *it is possible* is conveyed by the phrase *can
obtain*. Having made this change, I am inclined to
replace the indirect statement, *our investors can obtain*,
with the more direct *we can offer our investors*. This
change puts the real agent in the subject position.

2. In a recent survey it was revealed that 10% of graduating high school seniors are interested in a field of study
   we do not offer. This means that there is a group of at
   least 200,000 students that currently cannot consider
   our institution when selecting a college.

   Correction:

   A recent survey revealed that 10% of graduating
   high school seniors are interested in a field of study we
   do not offer. At least 200,000 students, therefore, cannot consider our institution when selecting a college.

   Explanation:

   The important corrections in this passage eliminate
   the expletives *it* and *there* to make the sentences more
   direct. Less important, but also helpful, is expressing
   the sense of *this means that* with the conjunctive adverb
   therefore (see guideline 6a).

3. There is evidence that this lack of balance has had a
   negative effect on retention of upper-level females, and
   there is a feeling among some that it would be
   desirable to have a more balanced female/male ratio.

   Correction:

   This lack of balance appears to lower the retention
   of upper-level females. Some feel a more balanced
   female/male ratio would be desirable.

   Explanation:

   Sometimes editing sentences to make them more

direct reveals that the sentences lack crucial information. The principal change here eliminates the indirect
statement *there is* twice. Notice, however, that when
the sentences are made more direct, we are left to wonder what the evidence is. I have eliminated the reference to evidence. We also wonder who wants a more
balanced female/male ratio. I have left the indefinite
some in the sentence because I can't be sure what
group it refers to. Making the sentences more direct
also reveals that the two ideas are not closely enough
related to be joined in a compound sentence.

4. There is a high demand for engineers that will
   continue to grow in the future.

   Correction:

   The demand for engineers is high and will grow
   higher in the future.

   Alternate correction:

   The already high demand for engineers will
   continue to grow in the future.

   Explanation:

   The first correction preserves the sense of the original sentence. The second correction assumes that the
   high demand for engineers has already been established. The context would determine which correction
   is preferable.

5. What are the forces that are responsible for the shifts
   in buying patterns? This is the question that pesters
   those in the industry who are charged with meeting
   consumer demand. While it is never possible to know
   what the causes are or what trends will prevail with
   certainty, it is a sure folly not to be aware of the patterns and not to try to anticipate the shifts.

   Correction:

   What forces cause the shifts in buying patterns?
   This question pesters those in the industry charged
   with meeting consumer demand. While we can never

know with certainty the causes or what trends will prevail, it is folly not to be aware of the patterns and anticipate the shifts.

Explanation:

Not all forms of *be* can be avoided. And sometimes the expletive *it* presents an idea better than any alternative construction. The writer's goal is not to eliminate such constructions completely but to cut down their frequency. Notice that in correcting the second sentence of the passage I have deleted *who are*, as guideline 7e suggests.

6. There is a feeling among the employees that the new hours will improve company morale.

Correction:

The employees feel the new hours will improve company morale.

Explanation:

Eliminating *there* results from a straightforward application of the guideline. The conjunction *that* introducing a subordinate clause can usually be eliminated without changing the meaning of the sentence.

7. It is always difficult for me to write the first sentence.

Correction:

I always find it difficult to write the first sentence.

Alternate correction:

I always find the first sentence difficult to write.

Explanation:

The first correction does not delete the expletive *it*, only moves it to a different position. The correction does, however, move the subject of the sentence to the natural subject position. The alternate correction eliminates the expletive, but changes the flavor of the sentence slightly. The two corrections illustrate that there is no right way to improve sentences.

8. Wherever there are oppressed citizens there is an unstable government.

Correction:

Where citizens are oppressed, government is unstable.

Explanation:

The corrected sentence violates two of the guidelines by including a passive construction and a form of *be*. The balance of the corrected sentence, however, justifies the violations.

9. We are the committee that decides which applicants will be on the final list.

Correction:

This committee decides which applicants will make the final list.

Alternate correction:

We decide as a committee which applicants will make the final list.

Explanation:

The alternate correction has a slightly different emphasis from the first. The context would determine which correction is preferable.

10. The bulletin outlining the new guidelines will be in the workroom and will be available for anyone who is planning to request a leave.

Correction:

The bulletin outlining the new guidelines will be in the workroom, available to anyone planning to request a leave.

Explanation:

This sentence could be trimmed further. The suggested correction only removes the repeated *will be*.

11. In this corner there are the dictionaries and the other reference works that will be helpful to those who are preparing reports.

Correction:

In this corner are the dictionaries and other reference works helpful to those preparing reports.

Explanation:

The principal offenders in this sentence are the phrases *that will be* and *who are*, covered in guideline 7e. The sentence is part of this exercise because it contains repeated *be* forms.

12. The new policy is that no one may smoke in the main lobby.

Correction:

According to the new policy, no one may smoke in the main lobby.

Alternate correction:

The new policy prohibits smoking in the main lobby.

Explanation:

The first correction does not shorten the sentences, only removes a form of *be*. The alternate correction is more direct, perhaps too direct. The writer would have to decide which correction is better.

4.   Prefer the more personal *you* and *I*.

1. Within the next few days all staff members in your department should complete the enclosed personalized forms in order to report their earned and unused vacation time as well as their accumulated sick leave as of May 31, 1992. The form requests information in the detail which is required for the university's annual financial reports and for implementation of a new payroll system this summer. Therefore, it is important that this office receive the information at an early date.

Correction:

Within a few days all staff members in your department should complete these personalized forms to report unused vacation time and accumulated sick leave as of May 31, 1992. The form requests information in the detail required for the university's annual financial reports and for implementing a new payroll system this summer. Please ask your staff members to return the completed forms soon.

Alternate correction:

Please ask all staff members in your department to report their unused vacation time and accumulated sick leave as of May 31, 1992. These personalized forms will help them provide the detailed information required for the university's annual financial reports and for the new payroll system we will install this summer. You can help us by having your staff members return the completed forms soon.

Explanation:

The first correction preserves the form and tone of the original request, but drops the bureaucratic *enclosed*. It also replaces the abstract nominalization *implementation* with the verb form *implementing*. The final sentence is recast as a direct request. The alternate correction personalizes the paragraph even further and replaces *implementing* with *installing*, which has a less official ring. Which of these revisions is suitable depends on the personality of the officer writing the request.

2. It would be difficult at this particular stage to even come close to telling you what the fee for the campaign itself would be. It will be based upon our findings, the geography in which the campaigns are to be conducted, the various kinds of program machinery that need to be set in order to assure that it will be a successful effort. Even though our fee is a flat fee and is not based upon a percentage, when a fee is looked at from a percentage viewpoint when the campaign is over, the percentages have run as low as five percent and as much as sixteen percent.

Correction:

At this stage we can't tell you the fee for the campaign. The fee will depend on our findings, the geography of the campaign, and the program machinery required for a successful effort. Although we charge a flat fee, not a percentage, in past campaigns our fees have ranged from five percent to sixteen percent.

Explanation:

The original paragraph, probably dictated, has the earmarks of spoken language: extra words, imprecise diction, and repetition. Just a little editing tightens the paragraph considerably without sacrificing information.

3. In the guide, typical writing problems are examined, and the cures for these problems are given through discussion and example. In many cases, options and alternatives are presented. An attempt is made, successfully it is hoped, to avoid direction by decree. Thus, the approach is more practical than academic. The aim of this guide is not to make writing more sophisticated (although it may become so) but to make it more direct, straightforward, and easy to follow and to help the writer develop a style that will reflect favorably on the work being reported or proposed.

Correction:

This guide examines typical writing problems and provides cures through discussion and example. Often it provides options and alternatives. The guide avoids direction by decree; its approach is more practical than academic. The aim is not to make writing more sophisticated (although it may become so) but to make writing more direct, straightforward, and easy to follow and in this way to help the writer develop a style that will reflect favorably on the work reported or proposed.

Alternate correction:

In this guide I examine typical writing problems and offer cures through discussion and example. Often I offer options and alternatives. I have tried to avoid direction by decree; my approach is more practical than academic. My aim is not to make your writing more sophisticated (although it may become so) but to make it more direct, straightforward and easy to follow. I want to help you develop a style that will reflect favorably on the work you report or propose.

Explanation:

The first correction sticks closely to the original, only converting the passive constructions to the active voice. It preserves the personification of the guide, suggesting that the guide attempts to improve the writer's style. The alternate correction presents the author of the guide as a teacher writing in the first person. The second paragraph may be too personal for a technical writing guide. But even the less personal style of the first correction avoids the implied anonymity of the passive voice.

5.   Use tense and person consistently.

1. The confusion over this renewal raises the question of what our policy had been before the new regulations were enacted.

Correction:

The confusion over this renewal raises the question of what our policy was before the new regulations were enacted.

Explanation:

Because the verb in the main clause is present, the verb in the second clause should be in the simple past form.

2. The employees are enjoying the refreshment center and have wondered what we did without it.

Correction:

The employees are enjoying the refreshment center and wonder what we did without it.

Explanation:

The *enjoying* and the *wondering* are going on at the same time. The tenses of the verbs should be the same.

3. Every student must have the work in on the day assigned. Don't be late.

Correction:

You must have your work in on the day assigned. Don't be late.

Alternate correction:

Every student must have the work in on the day assigned. None should be late (or: Late work will not be accepted).

Explanation:

For consistency both sentences must be addressed to the students in the second person, or both must refer to the students in the third person. The direct commands are more forceful, but they may seem too authoritarian.

4. One has to be familiar with the terrain before he can drive confidently.

Correction:

One has to be familiar with the terrain before one can drive confidently.

Alternate correction:

You must be familiar with the terrain before you can drive confidently.

Alternate correction:

To drive confidently one (you) must be familiar with the terrain.

Explanation:

The sentence is simple; the writer has several options to avoid mixing *one* and *he* or *one* and *you.*

5. Everyone should have your own copy of the employees' handbook. Employees should consult it for regulations regarding vacations, sick leave, and

personal time as well as arranged leaves of absence.
One can always get some time off if you need it.

Correction:

You should have your own copy of the employees'
handbook. Consult it for regulations regarding
vacations, sick leave, and personal time, as well as
arranged leaves of absence. You can always get some
time off it you need it.

Alternate correction:

Every employee should have a copy of the employees' handbook. Each should consult it for regulations
regarding vacations, sick leave, and personal time, as
well as arranged leaves of absence. An employee can
always get some time off if the need arises.

Explanation:

Rewriting the whole passage in the second person
and addressing the reader as *you* is the simplest
solution to the shifts in person in the original sentence.
The alternate correction keeps the tone impersonal,
but it requires the reader to be conscious of number
(singular or plural) as well as person.

6. Current openings are available on tape by calling the
job list number. Anyone interested in a particular
opening should go to the personnel office for an application form. Refer to the position by the code number
on the job list included on the tape.

Correction:

Current openings are available on tape. Call the job
list number. If you are interested in a particular opening,
go to the personnel office for an application form. Refer
to the position by the code number given on the tape.

Explanation:

In addition to shifting from third person to second
person, the original sentence includes a dangling element, the verb form *calling,* with no implied subject
and nothing to modify. In addition, it is not clear
whether *included* modifies *code number* or *job list*.

7. Career goals should incorporate more than one's salary and title.

Correction:

Your career goals should incorporate more than your salary and title.

Alternate correction:

A person's career goals should include more than salary and title.

Explanation:

The advisory tone of the sentence suggests that it would sound better in the form of instructions. The third person form of the sentence sounds stiff.

6.   Be careful with transitions.

1. The artist of the work is Edvard Munch, a Norwegian, and the painting was done between the years 1904 and 1907.

Correction:

The artist is Edvard Munch, a Norwegian. He painted the work between 1904 and 1907.

Alternate correction:

Edvard Munch, a Norwegian, painted the work between 1904 and 1907.

Explanation:

And expresses simple coordination. It does not indicate the connection between the two main clauses of the original sentence. The solution is either to separate the two clauses or to combine them in a single clause.

2. This screening process typically eliminates between 90% to 95% of all submitted properties.

Correction:

This screening process typically eliminates between 90% and 95% of all submitted properties.

Explanation:

Between requires the conjunction *and*, not the preposition *to*. If the first preposition were *from*, the writer could follow it with *to*.

3. I hope you will take a close look at the opportunity offered by Roger Breen, and if there are any questions that I can answer, please feel free to call.

Correction:

I hope you will take a close look at the opportunity offered by Roger Breen. If you have any questions I can answer, please feel free to call.

Explanation:

The relation between the sentences is not close enough for the conjunction *and*. I have tidied up the second sentence by removing *there are* and *that*.

4. Thank you for your continued interest and we will look forward to receiving your signed agreement soon.

Correction:

Thank you for your continued interest. We look forward to receiving your signed agreement soon.

Explanation:

The two sentences should be separated; the ideas are not coordinate. The verb in the second clause has been changed from future to present. *We look forward* implies the future without requiring a future verb.

5. By maintaining stiff standards my high school teacher was preparing me for college; although, I didn't appreciate it at the time.

Correction:

By maintaining stiff standards my high school teacher was preparing me for college although I didn't appreciate it at the time.

Alternate correction:

By maintaining stiff standards my high school

teacher was preparing me for college; however, I didn't appreciate it at the time.

Explanation:

In this case *although* is a subordinating conjunction. The clause it introduces should not be set off as a separate main clause. The alternate correction preserves the compound sentence by replacing *although* with a conjunctive adverb, *however*.

6. We have published a new biography that also covers the early years.

   Correction:

   We have published a new biography, and it, too, covers the early years.

   Alternate correction:

   We have published a new biography that covers the early years as well as the late years.

   Explanation:

   Also indicates something has been added. Whether a new biography has been added to cover the early years or whether the early years have been added to the coverage of the biograpy is not clear. To keep the possibilities separate requires recasting the sentence in two different ways.

7. Two new entrances have been opened on the west side of the building to ease congestion at peak hours. Employees will not be able to use these entrances during the early morning shift, however.

   Correction:

   Two new entrances have been opened on the west side of the building to ease congestion at peak hours. However, employees will not be able to use these entrances during the early morning shift.

   Explanation:

   Many writers think *however* loses its link to the previous clause and its contrastive function if it comes too late in the sentence, say after five or six words. Some authorities, uncomfortable placing *however* at the beginning of a sentence, would link the two clauses with a semicolon.

8. According to Freire, it seems as if he would like to totally change our concept of education completely.

   Correction:

   It seems Freire would like to change completely our concept of education.

   Explanation:

   Since Freire is the logical subject of the sentence, the transitional phrase *according to Freire* is not needed. *Totally* and *completely* are redundant modifiers.

9. The new spark plugs have a higher rating than the manual specifies, and thus you should use them only as a temporary solution.

   Correction:

   Because the new spark plugs have a higher rating than the manual specifies, you should use them only as a temporary solution.

   Explanation:

   Thus can mean *consequently* or *for this reason*. Strictly speaking the sentence is not wrong. But the relationship between the two main clauses is more clearly indicated by subordinating the first clause with *because*. The more common word is normally preferable.

10. It is not something that I do for anyone else, I continue education myself for my own benefit and satisfaction that I can accomplish what I set out to do.

    Correction:

    It is not something I do for anyone else; I continue education for my own benefit and to satisfy myself that I can accomplish what I set out to do.

    Explanation:

    Although *benefit* and *satisfaction* are parallel nouns, both cannot introduce the clause *that I can accomplish what I set out to do*. The two independent clauses require more than a comma to join them (see guideline 14a). I have removed *that* from the first clause simply because I can trim one word without any loss of meaning.

11. The deadline for this report is not far off, and we need to get together soon.

    Correction:

    Because the deadline for this report is not far off, we need to get together soon.

    Explanation:

    The two clauses are not coordinate. The first establishes the reason for the second.

12. The operator will add oil, so he needs to check the current level first.

    Correction:

    Before adding oil the operator should check the current level.

    Explanation:

    The temporal relation between the clauses, indicated by *first*, is more clearly indicated by starting the sentence with *before*.

7. Trim your style.

1. Modification of this statement reflecting her observations to the form of a question provides greater direction in developing the remainder of the steps of the research process.

   Correction:

   Restating her observations as a question helps her develop the remaining steps of her research.

   Explanation:

   Because the original sentence is obscure I have had to guess at the meaning. I can't be sure I have it right.

2. Experienced researchers, however, realize the concep-

tualization or development of the research question requires an ongoing literature review not only suggested by initial observation but also by the finalized question.

Correction:

Experienced researchers, however, realize that framing the research question requires the researcher to review the literature not only during initial observation but also as the final question is developed.

Explanation:

In recasting this sentence I have had to guess what the writer intended. Whether I have guessed correctly or not, I have at least trimmed some of the inflated language.

3. The preponderance of the more recent works have neglected to consider the historical context of the economic theory in the initial stages of its development.

Correction:

Most recent works have ignored the historical origins of the economic theory.

Explanation:

I take *the historical context . . . in the initial stages* to mean the historical origins. When the language is clogged with extraneous words, some guesswork is necessary.

4. Having utilized this technique in many analogous situations, I am cognizant of the benefits as well as the attendant risks.

Correction:

Having used this technique in similar situations, I am aware of the benefits as well as the risks.

Explanation:

With a little practice a writer or editor learns to spot inflated words such as *utilize* and *cognizant*.

5. General Operating Instructions are supplemented by

Specific Operating Instructions to which reference is necessary in order to operate an engine of a specific model and series. Specific Operating Instructions include specific procedures and information for a given engine series which may differ from that presented in the General Operating Instructions. Nevertheless, a working knowledge of the information presented in the General Operating Instructions is considered a necessary prerequisite to the use of the Specific Operating Instructions.

Correction:

General Operating Instructions are supplemented by Specific Operating Instructions. While the specific instructions for a model or series may differ from those presented in the General Operating Instructions, an understanding of the General Operating Instructions is necessary to use the Specific Operating Instructions.

Explanation:

The original version of this passage contains no grammatical errors. The improvement of the corrected version is in readability.

6. *Afterburner Nozzle Control Over-ride Switch*—Provision is made on some engines for a motor actuated, manually operated afterburner nozzle control over-ride. The afterburner nozzle control over-ride switch has two positions: OPEN and OFF. The over-ride will remain inoperative when the switch is in the OFF position. Should it be desirable for the pilot to select an "open" afterburner position during periods when the nozzle is normally closed, the over-ride switch may be moved to the OPEN position. This will cause the motor actuator to over-ride the nozzle control and hold the afterburner nozzle "open" as long as the switch remains in the OPEN position.

Correction:

Afterburner Nozzle Control Over-ride Switch—Some engines have a manually operated, but motor actuated, over-ride for the afterburner nozzle control.

The switch for this over-ride has two positions: OPEN and OFF. If the pilot selects an "open" position when the nozzle is normally closed, the motor actuator will over-ride the nozzle control and hold the nozzle open.

Explanation:

The string of nouns that heads this paragraph is probably useful to the operator of the aircraft even though it is hard to read. I have left it intact. In the body of the paragraph, however, I have done my best to unstack the noun phrases. To do so introduces some prepositions, but the improvement in readability justifies the changes. In my judgment the writer does not need to tell the operator that the over-ride will remain inoperative (will not function) when the switch is turned off.

7. Please utilize the means of egress to the rear.

    Correction:

    Please use the exit to the rear.

8. We must effect savings to the maximum extent possible.

    Correction:

    We must save as much as possible.

9. The full range of potential applications of this program is difficult to conceptualize.

    Correction:

    The many uses of this program are hard to imagine.

10. You may initiate the procedure whenever you deem it appropriate.

    Correction:

    You may start when you are ready.

11. Subsequent to her arrival, the manager commenced her perusal of applications.

    Correction:

    When she arrived, the manager looked at applications.

12. We will endeavor to secure the edition you have indicated on the request form.

    Correction:

    We will try to find the edition you requested.

13. Our compliance is contingent upon the timeliness of your reply.

    Correction:

    We will comply if you reply soon.

14. Our agent will inform you regarding what transpires at the annual meeting.

    Correction:

    Our agent will tell you what happens at the annual meeting.

7. Trim your style (additional exercises).

1. Last year the promotion committee prepared letters of inquiry for all those who had been through the promotion *process* during the previous five years. In general these people were asked to comment, in as much detail as they cared to, about their experience in the *process*. They were also invited to make evaluative comments about the *process* and to make recommendations, if they had any. The *process* of identifying those who should receive letters, distributing the letters, waiting for replies, and, finally, reading them was quite lengthy. That, plus the inability of the chair of the committee to continue the *process* toward the end of the year, is the reason that this year's committee has had to finish the project.

    Correction:

    Last year the promotion committee prepared letters of inquiry for all who had been through promotion during the previous five years. These people were asked to comment, in as much detail as they cared to, about their experience. They were also invited to evaluate the *process* and to make recommendations, if they had any. Identifying those who should receive letters, distributing the letters, waiting for replies, and, finally, reading the replies took a long time. Moreover, because the chair of the committee could not continue toward the end of the year, this year's committee has had to finish the project.

Explanation:

One instance of *process* remains. Notice that the passage has not been corrected as if it were wrong, simply tightened and streamlined.

2. The initial review of the literature essentially consists of a thorough search of all available studies related, in general, to the identified research question.

Correction:

The initial review of the literature is a search of all studies related to the research question.

3. A number of our members have written to express their frustration and disappointment with the fact that they are receiving multiple requests to join when they are already members.

Correction:

A number of our members have written to say they are annoyed by being asked repeatedly to join.

4. Computer science, mathematics, and physics are areas that are fundamental to any program in engineering.

Correction:

Computer science, mathematics, and physics are fundamental to an engineering program.

5. The fact that they perform well without the training does not mean they are performing at their maximum.

Correction:

That they perform well without the training does not mean they perform at their maximum.

6. A major issue in the field of computer engineering is that of defining the nature of the discipline.

   Correction:

   A major issue in computer engineering is defining the discipline.

7. These engines employ a can-annular type combustion chamber with a number of separate combustion liners or burners.

   Correction:

   These engines use a can-annular combustion chamber with several combustion liners or burners.

8. We would be pleased for you to contact each and every one of our clients since we have had a happy relationship with each one.

   Correction:

   Please contact any of our clients; we have had a happy relationship with each.

9. When the objects of study are cells and tissues far removed from a living body, there is often no compelling reason to address social, political, or moral issues related to human beings.

   Correction:

   When we study cells and tissues apart from a living body, we seldom need to address social, political, or moral issues.

10. We are definitely opposed to politicians who use their influence to amass wealth.

    Correction:

    We oppose politicians who use their influence to get rich.

11. Our warranty provides full and complete coverage during the first ninety days.

    Correction:

    Our warranty provides complete coverage for ninety days.

12. I came home absolutely exhausted after my first day as a volunteer.

    Correction:

    I came home exhausted after my first day as a volunteer.

13. It is our professional opinion that a plan could be developed that would be within your $10,000 budget and that your goals could be reached within a 45-day time frame.

    Correction:

    We believe we can develop a plan for under $10,000 and reach your goals within 45 days.

14. Homeowners who are developing a budget that will include home repairs face a task that is complicated.

    Correction:

    Homeowners developing a budget to include home repairs face a complicated task.

15. The exhibit is displayed in a large room which contains the individual inventions which have contributed to the development of the computer.

    Correction:

    The exhibit is in a large room containing the inventions that have contributed to the computer's development.

16. The evaluation process is a continuing one and part of the teaching method. As such, it can be used as a device for helping the student to gain security and a sense of direction through increased recognition of the positive and negative aspects of his/her performance.

    Correction:

    Evaluation is a continuing part of teaching. Evaluation helps students gain security and direction through recognition of the positive and negative aspects of their performance.

CHAPTER TWO: GUIDELINES FOR EDITING

8.   Use singular verbs with single subjects, plural verbs with plural subjects.

1. Each of the books we have chosen have soft covers.

   Correction:

   > Each of the books we have chosen has a soft cover.

   Explanation:

   > The grammatical subject is *each*, a singular indefinite pronoun.

2. The library's collection of government documents are housed in the library annex.

   Correction:

   > The library's collection of government documents is housed in the library annex.

   Explanation:

   > The grammatical subject is *collection*.

3. Neither of these arrangements present a satisfactory solution to our traffic problem.

   Correction:

   > Neither of these arrangements presents a satisfactory solution to our traffic problems.

   Explanation:

   > The grammatical subject is *neither*, a singular indefinite pronoun.

4. There's two good reasons for closing the office on Saturdays.

   Correction:

   > There are two good reasons for closing the office on Saturdays.

Explanation:

The grammatical subject, postponed by the expletive *there*, is *reasons*, a plural noun.

5. Every person in the office or all of them together have a chance to influence the choice of a new chief executive.

Correction:

None. The sentence is correct.

6. Hightower is one of the candidates who has endorsed the workers' compensation bill.

Correction:

Hightower is one of the candidates who have endorsed the workers' compensation bill.

Explanation:

The subject of *have* is *who*. *Who* agrees in number with its plural antecedent, *candidates*.

7. The conductor of the orchestra, along with six other musicians, (leaves/leave) for Germany next month.

Correction:

The conductor of the orchestra, along with six other musicians, leaves for Germany next month.

Explanation:

The phrase *along with six other musicians* is a parenthetical addition set off by commas. It does not affect the agreement between *conductor* and *leaves*. If *along with* were replaced by *and*, the commas would be removed and the grammatical subject would be plural.

8. All of the local union members and their national representative has signed the letter of complaint.

Correction:

All of the local union members and their national representative have signed the letter of complaint.

Explanation:

Compound subjects joined by *and* are treated as plural subjects.

9. None of the neighborhood residents were present at the City Council meeting.

   Correction:

   None of the neighborhood residents was present at the City Council meeting.

   Explanation:

   The grammatical subject is *none*, a singular indefinite pronoun.

10. A number of our newest acquisitions has already been checked out by students.

    Correction:

    A number of our newest acquisitions have already been checked out by students.

    Explanation:

    This correction sounds natural but appears to violate the rule of agreement. *Number* is a singular noun. In current usage, *a number* is so frequently taken to mean *a few* or *several* that most writers and readers treat it as a plural. Fowler suggests that when *number* has a definite article, *the*, it is singular; when *number* has an indefinite article, *a*, it is plural.

11. Along with a new baby comes a lot of choices.

    Correction:

    Along with a new baby come many choices.

    Explanation:

    Like *a number*, *a lot* is so frequently taken to be plural that it would be unnatural to use a singular verb. In correcting the sentence I have replaced *a lot of* with *many*, a clearly plural modifier. *Along* could be deleted, but I like the rhythm of the original sentence.

12. The faculty are divided on whether to support the proposed curriculum revision.

    Correction:

    The faculty is divided on whether to support the proposed curriculum revision.

Alternate correction:

Faculty members are divided on whether to support the proposed curriculum revision.

Explanation:

Strictly speaking, *faculty* refers to a single body made up of individual faculty members. The writer has a choice between treating *faculty* as singular or replacing it with the plural *faculty members*.

9. Avoid dangling and misplaced modifiers.

1. Before entering college, my mother often told me college would be the best years of my life.

   Correction:

   Before I entered college, my mother often told me college would be the best years of my life.

   Explanation:

   It is possible that the writer's mother made this remark before the mother entered college, but it is more likely that the implied subject of *entering* is the person referred to as *me*.

2. As an individual investing your own hard earned dollars, we think you'll be interested in what our company has to offer.

   Correction:

   Because you are investing your own hard earned dollars, we think you'll be interested in what our company has to offer.

   Explanation:

   Because the implied subject of the introductory phrase must be the same as the grammatical subject of the sentence, *as an individual* appears to modify *we*. If we change the introductory phrase to a clause with its own subject and predicate, it no longer has to modify the subject of the main clause.

3. While difficult to quantify, it seems obvious that our image as a major university would be enhanced by an engineering program of high quality.

   Correction:

   Although an image is difficult to quantify, our image as a major university would be enhanced by an engineering program of high quality.

   Explanation:

   The dangling modifier is corrected by converting the introductory phrase to a clause. When the sentence is recast to avoid the expletive *it*, the sense of the phrase *it is obvious* seems superfluous.

4. Come and see Rick Waters. There are no attorney's fees unless successful.

   Correction:

   Come and see Rick Waters. You will pay no attorney's fees unless you are successful.

   Explanation:

   Advertisements are often deliberately vague. What constitutes success for a client dealing with an attorney is not clear. The advertiser probably does not want to be specific.

5. By thumbing the "great authors" day and night, absorbing their thoughts, relishing their words, their expertise and ideals will become the student's.

   Correction:

   By thumbing the great authors day and night, absorbing their thoughts, relishing their words, the student will acquire their expertise and ideals.

   Explanation:

   Recasting the main clause so that its grammatical subject is the same as the implied subject of the introductory phrases is simple. Correcting the grammar of the sentence does not clarify its meaning. The quotation marks around *great authors* are scare quotes covered in the chapter on punctuation.

6. We are not an elitist university. We seek to attract talented students who are capable of taking on society's important challenges, however.

   Correction:

   We are not an elitist university. We seek, however, to attract talented students capable of taking on society's challenges.

   Alternate correction:

   We are not an elitist university; however, we seek to attract talented students capable of taking on society's challenges.

   Explanation:

   However makes the link between the two sentences or the two main clauses. At the end of the second sentence *however* is too remote to make the proper connection. Some authorities argue that it is wrong to begin a sentence with *however*. These same authorities would argue that it is wrong to begin a sentence with a coordinating conjunction, such as *but* or *and*. While I don't accept their arguments, I have avoided starting a sentence with *however* just because I have that option as an editor. In truth, whether I link the main clauses with a semicolon or whether I end the first sentence with a period after *university* and start *however* with a capital letter is a matter of small stylistic significance.

7. We'll have to do what counts most first and accept that we must put off what doesn't touch our lives directly until later.

   Correction:

   We'll have to do first what counts most and accept that we must put off until later what doesn't touch our lives directly.

   Explanation:

   The adverbial phrase *until later* is out of place; it seems to modify *touch* rather than *put off*. Moving *until later* to its proper place after *put off* makes the corresponding shift, placing *first* after *do*, seem natural and right. I make the second change reluctantly; I like the rhythm of *do what counts most first*.

8. By putting the rebellion in its historical setting and examining the economic conditions of the time, it becomes clear that more was at stake than personal freedom or individual rights.

   Correction:

   By putting the rebellion in its historical setting and examining the economic conditions of the time, we make it clear that more was at stake than personal freedom or individual rights.

   Alternate correction:

   By putting the rebellion in its historical setting and examining the economic conditions of the time, we discover that more than personal freedom or individual rights was at stake.

   Explanation:

   In both corrections the grammatical subject of the main clause is *we*, the implied subject of the introductory phrase. Once we have made that change and corrected the dangling modifier, we can tinker with the rest of the main clause.

9. Through careful negotiations with management, some improvement of the office conditions under which we work may be achieved.

   Correction:

   Through careful negotiations with management, we can achieve some improvement in our office conditions.

   Explanation:

   The essential change here is to correct the dangling modifier by making the grammatical subject of the main clause the same as the implied subject of the introductory phrase. The other changes are intended to tighten the main clause.

10. Erosion of the soil around the foundation may create conditions that cause walls to crack slowly.

    Correction:

    Erosion of the soil around the foundation may slowly create conditions that cause walls to crack.

    Explanation:

    The writer may have intended to suggest that under certain conditions walls crack slowly. If so, then I have changed the meaning of the sentence with my correction. But if the writer meant that walls crack slowly, it would be better to risk a split infinitive, *to slowly crack*, and thus eliminate the ambiguity of the original sentence.

11. The supplemental pages include procedures for installing the new control devices which may be different from the ones you are using.

    Correction:

    The supplemental pages include procedures for installing the new control devices. These procudures may be different from the ones you are using.

    Alternate correction:

    The supplemental pages include procedures for installing the new control devices, which may be different from the control devices you are using.

    Explanation:

    The confusion in this sentence arises from the ambiguous modifying phrase. Nothing in the sentence tells us whether the procedures are different or the control devices are different. The context would determine which reading is correct.

12. Carrying a stack of plates, balanced precariously, the waiter turned the corner on one foot.

    Correction:

    Carrying a precariously balanced stack of plates, the waiter turned the corner on one foot.

Alternate correction:

Carrying a stack of plates, the waiter, balanced precariously, turned the corner on one foot.

Explanation:

The original sentence is perfectly ambiguous; *balanced precariously* can modify in either direction. Such ambiguity might be an asset in poetry. In straightforward prose, it is not.

13. The crowd greeted the candidate as she entered the hall, chanting, "Four more years!"

Correction:

Greeting the candidate as she entered the hall, the crowd chanted, "Four more years!"

Explanation:

If the candidate was shouting, "Four more years!" the sentence would have to be revised differently.

10.   Choose the proper pronoun.

1. When I went home to visit, I felt like a person that had been transformed without knowing it.

Correction:

When I went home to visit, I felt like a person who had been transformed without knowing it.

Alternate correction:

When I went home to visit, I felt I had been transformed without knowing it.

Explanation:

The offender in the original sentence is *that* used to refer to a person. The second correction is tighter but may not fit the context as well as the first.

2. Stephen Jobs applied Quantitative Management Theory to Apple Computer, Inc. This was important to apply, especially in the computer industry, because it is dynamic and complex.

Correction:

Stephen Jobs applied Quantitative Management Theory to Apple Computer, Inc. This was an important move because the computer industry is dynamic and complex.

Alternate correction:

Stephen Jobs applied Quantitative Management Theory to Apple Computer, Inc. The application of this dynamic and complex theory was important to the computer industry.

Explanation:

The two corrections convey different interpretations of the ambiguous original sentence. I can't be sure which interpretation was intended.

3. With the advent of the printing press, readers had a greater sense of contact with writers which heightened their interest.

Correction:

With the advent of the printing press, the interest of readers was heightened by a greater sense of contact with writers.

Explanation:

Which appears to refer to *a greater sense of contact*. If it refers to *writers*, the proper pronoun is *who*.

4. Disembarking onto the beautiful white sand of Gardner Bay, a group of seven travelers and myself, with our naturalist guide, made our way along the beach.

Correction:

Disembarking onto the beautiful white sand of Gardner Bay, a group of seven travelers and I, with our naturalist guide, made our way along the beach.

Alternate correction:

Disembarking onto the beautiful white sand of Gardner Bay, a group of travelers that included me and our naturalist guide made our way along the beach.

Explanation:

While the sentence can be recast to make *I* the proper pronoun, *myself* is out of place unless the action is reflexive.

5. Who do you expect to finish the race first?

Correction:

Whom do you expect to finish the race first.

Explanation:

An analysis of the syntax of this sentence reveals that *whom* is the subject of an infinitive phrase and belongs in the object form. Rewriting the sentence clarifies the grammatical function of *whom*: *You do expect whom to finish the race.* Some writers would argue that *who* is always proper at the beginning of a sentence.

6. The group of senators which had opposed this bill found themselves embarrassed by its defeat.

Correction:

The group of senators who had opposed this bill found themselves embarrassed by its defeat.

Alternate correction:

The senators who opposed this bill found themselves embarrassed by its defeat.

Explanation:

I prefer the alternate correction as less wordy than the first correction. I have included the first, however, so that I could deal with whether the relative pronoun (*who* or *which*) modifies *group* or *senators*. It doesn't matter, anyway. Both *group* and *senators* would be regarded as human referents.

7. The committee appointed to work on employee benefits spent their time handling individual grievances.

Correction:

The committee appointed to work on employee benefits spent its time handling individual grievances.

Explanation:

Collective nouns such as *group* and *committee, army, class,* or *team,* may be regarded as singular or plural, according to the intentions of the writer. The original sentence, therefore, is not wrong. I have corrected it to suggest a singular sense because I want to distinguish between the time a committee would have together and any other time the committee members might have as individuals.

8. You can pick whoever you like. Any of our trainees can do the work.

Correction:

You can pick whomever you like. Any of our trainees can do the work.

Explanation:

Whomever is the object of *like,* not of *pick.* The objective form is appropriate in either case.

9. Once you have enrolled with our company, you will be assigned a representative that will make an appointment to discuss the benefits.

Correction:

Once you have enrolled with our company, you will be assigned a representative who will make an appointment to discuss the benefits.

Explanation:

The representative is human; the proper pronoun is *who* whether the modifying clause is regarded as restrictive or nonrestrictive. I take the clause as restrictive and therefore have not set it off with a comma. Another writer may feel the clause is nonrestrictive and add a comma after *representative.* The difference is real, but either interpretation is allowable.

10. Mr. Mendez was able to talk with the senator because he happened to come through the door at just the right moment.

Correction:

Mr. Mendez was able to talk with the senator because the senator happened to come through the door at just the right moment.

Explanation:

It is impossible to tell from the original sentence whether the person entering at the right moment was the senator or Mr. Mendez.

11. For students field learning has always received high marks and been viewed as a key element in their social work education. As such, field education is one of the essential elements in each student's learning experience. Because it occupies such an important place, field education is the focus for many of the issues which confront the relationship between social work education and social work practice. The relationship of the two systems is essential for field learning which is educationally directed. Because of its importance, the field is a charged area for both practice and education.

Correction:

Field learning has always received high marks from students, who regard it as an essential element in their social work education. Because it occupies an important place in each student's learning, field education is the focus for many issues that confront the relationship between social work education and social work practice. The relationship of education and practice is essential for educational field learning, which in turn is a charged area for both practice and education.

Explanation:

I can't be sure I have captured everything in the original paragraph.

11. Avoid separating subject and verb.

1. My sister, when she discovered the fire ants, tried to call off the picnic.

   Correction:

   When my sister discovered the fire ants, she tried to call off the picnic.

2. The new publishing company, because it produces mainly manuals and catalogues, will not attract many literary figures.

   Correction:

   Because the new publishing company produces mainly manuals and catalogues, it will not attract many literary figures.

   Alternate correction:

   The new publishing company will not attract many literary figures; it produces mainly manuals and catalogues.

   Explanation:

   Once the two clauses are disentangled so that one doesn't interrupt the other, the writer has a good deal of freedom in arranging the clauses to vary the emphasis.

3. Evelyn, seeing the auditorium packed with parents and friends, panicked and forgot her speech.

   Correction:

   Seeing the auditorium packed with parents and friends, Evelyn panicked and forgot her speech.

   Explanation:

   Although *seeing the auditorium packed with parents and friends* is a participial phrase modifying *Evelyn*, it has adverbial force and sounds better at the beginning of the sentence.

4. The excited children, clapping and cheering, burst through the schoolroom door.

Correction:

The excited children burst through the schoolroom door, clapping and cheering.

Alternate correction:

The excited children burst clapping and cheering through the schoolroom door.

Explanation:

This sentence also illustrates that participles often have adverbial force.

5. "The Great Emancipator," which is the name some historians gave to Abraham Lincoln, was assassinated during his second term of office.

Correction:

Abraham Lincoln, called "The Great Emancipator," was assassinated during his second term of office.

Explanation:

The original sentence is grammatically flawed. The subject of the main clause is the name, not the man. In the correction I have left a modifying phrase between the subject and the verb, but the intervening phrase modifies the subject and is therefore not intrusive.

6. Students, who often may be oppressed by deadlines, are tempted to seek out publishing companies that produce term papers.

Correction:

Students oppressed by deadlines are often tempted to seek out publishing companies that produce term papers.

Explanation:

In revising the sentence I have made the adjective phrase *oppressed by deadlines* restrictive. This change alters the sense of the sentence; it now implies that only students oppressed by deadlines are tempted to seek out publishers of term papers. This more charitable statement is indicated by the auxiliary verb *may*.

7. Rodney Buckford, the new shortstop, has been an important addition to our team.

    Correction:

    None.

8. Rodney Buckford, in the season opener, hit a homerun.

    Correction:

    In the season opener Rodney Buckford hit a homerun.

    Explanation:

    Sentences 7 and 8 illustrate that an adjective phrase modifying the subject is acceptable between subject and verb, but an adverbial phrase modifying the verb is better shifted to the beginning of the sentence.

12.   Keep coordinate elements in parallel form.

1. Women had to limit what they said, did, or write in order to succeed.

    Correction:

    Women had to limit what they said, did, or wrote in order to succeed.

2. Early in the epidemic, what attitude to take towards AIDS patients and what language chosen to describe them became matters of debate.

    Correction:

    Early in the epidemic, what attitude to take towards AIDS patients and what language to choose in describing them became matters of debate.

    Explanation:

    Changing the form of *chosen* to the infinitive *to choose* so that it will be parallel with *to take* requires that I change the form of *to describe* so that it will not be parallel. The verb forms should reflect the syntactic structure of the sentence.

3. Such rapid development in knowledge serves as an example of the ability of "good research" to target and then work quickly and efficiently to solve tragic human problems.

Correction:

Such rapid development in knowledge serves as an example of the ability of "good research" to target tragic human problems and then to work quickly and efficiently at solving them.

Explanation:

The revision adjusts the verb forms so that *to target* and *to work* are parallel. In this sentence, as in sentence 2, it is advisable to alter the modifying infinitive, in this case *to solve*, so that it does not appear to be a third infinitive in a series. I have also moved the object of the infinitive verbs to a position after *to target*. I see no gain in emphasis in leaving the object at the end of the sentence.

4. A few preliminary cautions will help to avoid trouble: (1) the optimum temperature for the CRT terminal is between 65 and 75 degrees; (2) don't allow the terminal to be operated excessively; (3) the terminal is not mobile and should not be moved; (4) due to the sensitivity of the machine, no smoking is allowed near the terminal.

Correction:

A few preliminary cautions will help to avoid trouble: (1) the optimum temperature for the CRT terminal is between 65 and 75 degrees; (2) the terminal should not be operated excessively; (3) the terminal is not mobile and should not be moved; (4) because the machine is sensitive, no smoking is allowed near the terminal.

Explanation:

In revising this sentence I was tempted to put the cautions in imperative form: *Do not operate the terminal excessively; Do not smoke;* and so on. I put the cautions in the gentler declarative form because the writer calls them cautions, not warnings. The only firm requirement is that the cautions be in parallel form. In changing *due to* to *because* I have humored my old-fashioned conviction that *due* is an adjective and must modify a noun. I wouldn't insist on this change if the writer wanted to retain *due to*.

5. As the examination of the major rhetoricians progresses, we will consider historical setting, the educational reforms undertaken by each man, the prevailing political and social climate, and we shall ask how and why cultural literacy and rhetoric were important in each instance.

   Correction:

   As the examination of the major rhetoricians progresses, we shall consider historical setting, we shall examine the educational reforms undertaken by each man and assess the prevailing political and social climate, and we shall ask how and why cultural literacy and rhetoric were important in each instance.

   Explanation:

   In making the series of clauses parallel, I have converted a four-part series to a three-part series with one of the elements divided. This modification is not necessary, but I felt the reader would appreciate some relief in a long and complicated sentence. Looking closely at the verbs, I noticed the writer shifted the auxiliary form between *will consider* and *shall ask*. As recently as fifty years ago grammarians clung to a distinction between *shall* and *will*, using *shall* for the first person, *will* for second and third. While most writers regard the rule about *shall* and *will* as obsolete, it is still wise to be consistent—to keep the forms parallel, at least within a single sentence.

6. Of course there are men upon whom the burdens of divorce and the sacrifices required to raise children have fallen or been taken on with equal weight.

Correction:

Of course there are men who have assumed the burdens of divorce and the sacrifices required to raise children or have shared them equally.

Explanation:

In modifying this sentence I have surrendered the
metaphor of the burdens falling upon the men. The
need to put the predicates in parallel form was greater
than the attraction of the figure of speech. Once the
metaphor was abandoned, the modifier *with equal
weight* no longer made sense.

7. The stasis theory gave those unschooled in dialectic a
   starting point from which to begin a successful
   dialogue either with a person or a text.

   Correction:

   The stasis theory gave those unschooled in dialectic
   a starting point from which to begin a successful dialogue with either a person or a text.

   Alternate correction:

   The stasis theory gave those unschooled in dialectic
   a starting point from which to begin a successful dialogue either with a person or with a text.

   Explanation:

   What follows *or* must have the same grammatical
   structure as what follows *either*. The ability of the computer to move or copy the preposition *with* makes this
   sentence easy to correct.

8. Cultivating audience awareness allowed Luther and
   his contemporaries to prove not only the inconsistencies in the claims made by the Church, but to unite the
   common folk in a way previously unknown.

   Correction:

   Cultivating audience awareness allowed Luther and
   his contemporaries not only to prove the inconsistencies
   in the claims made by the Church, but also to unite
   the common folk in a way previously unknown.

Explanation:

What follows *but* must have the same grammatical structure as what follows *not only*. Having made this change, I felt the sentence would be clearer if I added *also*.

9. Printing allowed easier circulation of ideas, adaptation of those ideas to a new historical context, and opened the door to new study methods as students began to own their own copies of important texts.

Correction:

Printing allowed easier circulation of ideas, adaptation of those ideas to a new historical context, and the development of new study methods as students began to own copies of important texts.

Alternate correction:

Printing allowed ideas to circulate, adapted to a new historical context, and opened the door to new study methods as students began to own copies of important texts.

Explanation:

The first correction creates a series of nominalizations, following guideline 12 but violating guideline 1b. In the alternate correction I have combined the first two elements of the series. Inevitably, editing sentences changes their meaning slightly. I have deleted *their own* because the idea is conveyed by the verb *own*.

10. A formal organization of any kind has both a structure and a set of procedures, both formal and informal, which deal with the decision-making process, getting the work done, informing people about what is happening, establishment of accountability, and affirming rules or guidelines for interaction between persons.

Correction:

A formal organization of any kind has a structure and a set of procedures, formal and informal. Both structure and procedures contribute to decision making, getting the work done, informing people about what is happening, establishing accountability, and affirming guidelines for interaction between persons.

Explanation:

The original sentence does not establish whether both structure and procedures have a part in decision making, getting the work done, and the rest or whether accomplishing the multiple goals is the function of the procedures only. In saying both structure and procedures contribute, I am imposing my interpretation on the sentence. I must make a choice. I have left one ambiguity intact; I can't be sure whether *formal and informal* modifies both *structure* and *set of procedures* or whether only the procedures are formal and informal. I think it is the latter, but the sentence does not depend on clarifying the ambiguity.

13.   Avoid the most damaging spelling errors.

1. When the bell sounds, (its/it's) time to close the door.

   Correction:

   When the bell sounds, it's time to close the door.

2. This engine seems to have (its/it's) own personality.

   Correction:

   This engine seems to have its own personality.

3. The touring players found (there/their) way to the center of town.

   Correction:

   The touring players found their way to the center of town.

4. If (there/their) are any new books in, you'll find them in a box by the door.

   Correction:

   If there are any new books in, you'll find them in a box by the door.

The sentence could be better:

    If we have any new books, you'll find them in a box by the door.

5. We are all (to/too) tired to try again.

    Correction:

    We are all too tired to try again.

6. The child swam (to/too) the raft and back.

    Correction:

    The child swam to the raft and back.

7. Mr. Elroy, (to/too), will attend the service.

    Correction:

    Mr. Elroy, too, will attend the service.

8. I want to know (whose/who's) baseball glove is on the back porch.

    Correction:

    I want to know whose baseball glove is on the back porch.

9. Please let the office know (whose/who's) going to greet the new employees.

    Correction:

    Please let the office know who's going to greet the new employees.

10. You'll have to answer (your/you're) own phone.

    Correction:

    You'll have to answer your own phone.

11. If (your/you're) ready to begin, turn to page three in (your/you're) text booklet.

    Correction:

    If you're ready to begin, turn to page three in your test booklet.

12. We like to (here/hear) success stories.

    Correction:

    We like to hear success stories.

13. (Here/Hear) now, what are you doing with that book?

Correction:

Here now, what are you doing with that book?

Explanation:

Some readers may prefer to use *hear* in this situation. If the word were moved to the end of the sentence, some writers would say,

Tell me what you are doing with that book, hear?

14.   Pay attention to conspicuous comma errors.

1. The average man's definition of himself does not include the wants of women, therefore, he concludes that he does not understand women.

Correction:

The average man's definition of himself does not include the wants of women; therefore, he concludes that he does not understand women.

2. I will be out of my office next week so you will not be able to come for a conference.

Correction:

I will be out of my office next week, so you will not be able to come for a conference.

Explanation:

In this sentence *so* is used as a coordinating conjunction roughly equivalent to *therefore*. This usage is informal but acceptable in most contexts.

3. Piaget's studies with children brought him recognition as a child psychologist, he is the world's acknowledged expert in the area of cognitive development.

Correction:

Piaget's studies with children brought him recognition as a child psychologist. He is the world's acknowledged expert in the area of cognitive development.

Explanation:

Although I have broken the sentence into two, the writer could as acceptably treat the two clauses as coordinate and separate them with a semicolon.

4. Literature is a social institution, Plato in effect affirmed, as such it must be judged by social standards.

Correction:

Literature is a social institution, Plato in effect affirmed; as such it must be judged by social standards.

Alternate correction:

Literature is a social institution, Plato believed, and it must be judged by social standards.

Explanation:

The first correction handles only the punctuation of the original sentence. The second correction eliminates the bureaucratic sound of *in effect* and *as such*.

5. Some feelings are kindled only to smoulder away and leave dead ashes, others tend to kindle on and on, awakening thought, rousing to vigorous action.

Correction:

Some feelings are kindled only to smoulder away and leave dead ashes; others kindle on and on, awakening thought, rousing to vigorous action.

Explanation:

Punctuating the sentence is easier than curbing the headlong metaphor. I have left the metaphor intact because a writer is entitled to such flourishes. I have eliminated *tend to* as one of those empty additions covered in guidelines 7b and 7c. I have overlooked an awkward shift from the passive *are kindled* to the active *kindle*. To remove this shift I would have to recast the sentence entirely.

6. Persuasion, according to the sophists, fails to consider the interests of the hearer.

Frequently it even assails them.

In fact the sophistic precepts imply the hearer's part in discourse is spoiled.

Correction:

According to the sophists, persuasion fails to consider the interests of the hearer; frequently it even assails them. In fact, the sophistic precepts imply the hearer's part in discourse is spoiled.

Explanation:

The context of these sentences might suggest that the sentence should begin with *persuasion*, for rhetorical emphasis. Not having the context to help, I have moved the adverb modifier in accordance with guideline 11.

7. Your resume should make you sound like an achiever.

Forget your negative aspects.

Stress your positive attributes.

Correction:

Your resume should make you sound like an achiever. Forget your negative aspects, stress your positive attributes.

Explanation:

The second and third sentences could be joined with a semicolon. I have chosen to use a comma because the two clauses are brief, closely linked, and parallel in form.

8. The participants are to remain anonymous.

They should use only their assigned numbers on the form.

They should not sign the form.

Correction:

The participants are to remain anonymous. They should use only their assigned numbers and should not sign the form.

9. My own writing takes me by surprise.

I don't know what I will say until I say it.

I don't know what I have said until I hear it.

Correction:

My own writing takes me by surprise: I don't know what I will say until I say it or what I have said until I hear it.

Explanation:

I have used the colon in a slightly unconventional way. Because the second and third sentences expand on the first, explaining what it means, I think the colon is justified. Some writers would replace the colon with a period.

10. In my opinion this is not merely a good book.

It is a great book.

It cannot fail to make its mark.

Correction:

In my opinion this is not merely a good book but a great book. It cannot fail to make its mark.

Explanation:

Although other ways of combining these sentences are possible, I have chosen to break the sentence after *a great book.* I want to emphasize the phrase by putting it at the end of a sentence.

11. Honestly I can't understand your position on mandatory insurance.

Correction:

Honestly, I can't understand your position on mandatory insurance.

Explanation:

In my judgment, *honestly* modifies the whole sentence and tells how the statement is intended. If *honestly* is a true adverb, modifying understand, it should be moved to the spot before *understand.*

12. I can't honestly support your position on mandatory insurance.

Correction:

None. Here *honestly* modifies the verb.

13. A ballplayer preoccupied with her batting average risks sacrificing the team's success for her own glory.

    Correction:

    None. Unless there is a reason to add a comma, don't.

14. The desire to solve all problems and to answer all questions was more than a vague dream of these early scientists.

    Correction:

    None.

15. After a quick survey of the list of authors in the third chapter she was able to locate the quotation.

    Correction:

    After a quick survey of the list of authors in the third chapter, she was able to locate the quotation.

    Explanation:

    The comma makes clear that *in the third chapter* modifies *list of authors* and not the main verb of the sentence.

16. Before examining these samples I want to verify the location of the accident.

    Correction:

    None.

    Explanation:

    Whether to put a comma after *samples* is a judgment call.

17. To be frank your explanation of the process is difficult to follow.

    Correction:

    To be frank, your explanation of the process is difficult to follow.

Explanation:

> *To be frank* modifies the whole sentence.

18. Again I apologize for my delay in getting this tape to you.

    Correction:

    > None.

    Explanation:

    > A comma after *again* would indicate that *again* is a sentence modifier. Because I choose to treat *again* as an adverb modifying *apologize*, I have left out the comma.

19. Every one of the students on this chart has met the composition requirements of our college.

    Correction:

    > None.

    Alternate correction:

    > Every student on this chart has met the composition requirements of our college.

    Explanation:

    > The punctuation of the original sentence is correct. Because the sentence is long, the writer might be tempted to insert a comma after *chart*, needlessly separating subject and predicate. With the sentence rewritten to streamline the subject noun phrase, the writer would be less tempted to add an unnecessary comma.

20. Hopefully every person we have asked to participate will return the data card before the closing date.

    Correction:

    > Hopefully, every person we have asked to participate will return the data card before the closing date.

    Explanation:

    > *Hopefully* is a usage bugaboo, a pariah among adverbs, in my judgment needlessly maligned. Seen as

a sentence modifier, *hopefully* is no more out of place than *frankly*, which most purists do not reject. Because some readers object to *hopefully* used in this way, I avoid it in my own writing. But I do not correct my students who use it.

CHAPTER THREE: PUNCTUATION

In presenting the corrections for the exercises on punctuation, I have not repeated the original sentences. In most of the corrected sentences the words remain the same. The punctuation of the sentences generally requires no explanation. From time to time I have commented on alternative options.

Essentials

15.   Punctuate the end of a sentence with a period, a question mark, or an exclamation point.

1. Thank you for attending our banquet for the retiring staff members.

2. Congratulations. I was pleased to see an employee of DataCorp win the award.

3. How generous you are. I will treasure your gift.
   Explanation:

   A writer might prefer an exclamation point after the first sentence. Whether a period or an exclamation point is better would depend on the context of the sentence. The exclamation point is a bit flamboyant for a business letter, but might be appropriate in a personal letter.

4. I want to know if you have finished the report you were working on.

5. What kind of loyalty is this, when an employee walks out after twelve years for the first offer that comes along?

   Explanation:

   Whether this sentence should end with a period or a question mark depends on whether the writer feels it is a true question or a rhetorical comment in the form of a question.

6. Stop your bickering! I can't stand distractions when I am working.

7. Tell me, how do you plan to respond to the institute's request?

   Explanation:

   Although grammatically this sentence is an imperative, *tell me*, and the question is embedded as a subordinate clause, the rhetorical force of the sentence is that of a question. The opening clause is punctuated as if it were a sentence modifier.

8. He doesn't understand why he has to remind his wife to plan their anniversary; after all, that's her responsibility not his.

   Explanation:

   This sentence could as easily be punctuated as two sentences.

9. Where are the volunteers, I want to know?

   Explanation:

   Whether this is a declarative sentence ending with a period or an interrogative sentence ending with a question mark depends on how the writer wants the reader to perceive it. In this sentence, as in sentence 7, the writer can punctuate according to the rhetorical force of the question, *where are the volunteers?* or according to the grammatical form of the statement, *I want to know.*

10. It's no longer a question of who will manage the accounts; it is now an issue of who will make company policy.

    Explanation:

    The declarative force of this sentence displaces its grammatically interrogative form.

11. The story of Chief Joseph and his doomed people raises many questions. Why did the U. S. Army insist on treating the Indians the way it did? Were the white settlers justified in taking the Indians' territory?

    Explanation:

    The writer might put a colon after *questions* to anticipate the series that follows. Because the series includes only two questions, I have not regarded the questions as a restatement of the phrase *many questions*.

12. The health care system of this country is a staggering enterprise, in any sense of the adjective. Whatever the failures of distribution and lack of coordination, it is the gigantic scale and scope of the total collective effort that first catches the breath, and the cost. [Thomas, p. 36]

    Explanation:

    I have provided the punctuation that Lewis Thomas uses for this sentence in *The Medusa and the Snail*. If it were my sentence, I would probably separate the final three words, *and the cost*, with a dash.

16.   Follow the rules governing commas.

1. This year, because of the larger enrollments, we are offering the course at several times.

    Explanation:

    By putting a comma after *year*, I have treated the two introductory modifiers as independent of each other.

2. We have many pairs of skates, but none in your size.

3. Chief Joseph was a peaceful, honorable man who loved his land and his people.

Explanation:

The comma after *peaceful* suggests that *peaceful* and *honorable* are equal modifiers of man.

4. Although the examples in this exercise are crafted for the occasion, they could as easily have been drawn from published sources.

5. After the glamor of traveling to exotic locales, how will she adjust to the ordinary day-by-day of a home office job?

Explanation:

The hyphens in *day-by-day* make it a compound noun. Without the hyphens the sentence would be confusing.

6. Under the new regulations we will not be able to use the application form we used to.

7. The asters comprise a very large genus, there being more than 650 species from nearly all parts of the world except Australia. [Roadside Flowers of Texas, p. 228]

Explanation:

The added phrase beginning with *there being* is grammatically an absolute phrase with no specific word to modify. It is punctuated as an added parenthetical element.

8. Our report is not ready because we were unable to complete the telephone survey, as scheduled, in May.

Explanation:

The commas setting off *as scheduled* make the phrase parenthetical. Without the commas, *in May* would appear to modify *scheduled* rather than *to complete*.

9. Course offerings vary from site to site. They include a self-paced, individualized sequence covering arithmetic/pre-algebra/algebra, reading the classics, basics of writing, Latin for language development, mathematical problem solving, and science exploration. [Flexible Pacing for Able Learners, p. 57]

10. We start with the belief that the best education takes place when new concepts, new content, are presented in a way and at a pace that fits diverse learning rates and learning styles.

    Explanation:

    By setting off *new content* as an appositive, I am treating it as parenthetical. The verb, *are presented*, therefore agrees with *concepts*, a plural.

11. In fact, his foolish behavior could land him in court.

    Explanation:

    The comma after *in fact* suggests the phrase is a sentence modifier.

12. Fortunately, today more and more people are aware of the benefits of recycling; however, some neanderthals will always clog our landfills with reusable paper and cans.

    Explanation:

    Some writers would put *neanderthals* in quotation marks. I prefer not to call attention to the metaphor in that way. Having chosen to call such persons *neanderthals*, I must do so confidently.

13. Among Dalworth, National, and Lane, Sewell ranks Dalworth first in terms of revenue paid for transportation. Sewell uses National least because of National's history of late deliveries, equipment not being available, and Sewell's perception that on-time deliveries are not important to National.

    Explanation:

    In repunctuating this sentence I must look closely to discover why the original writer changed the order of the three names of trucking firms. Close inspection reveals no sound reason to change the order—in fact, no sound reason to repeat the series. I can eliminate the series and at the same time tighten the sentence by recasting it in the active form.

14. The absence of any evidence showing that the grant of these applications would cause hardship to competi-

tors or interfere with services they are now rendering presents good cause to grant these applications.

Explanation:

Although this sentence is long and cumbersome, no rule justifies putting in commas. A comma after *rendering*, where a reader might pause for breath, would separate the subject from the verb. In editing the sentence I deleted the *which* following *services*.

15. Particularly at those schools where scheduling has been arranged in blocks to permit an easy flow of students from group to group studying the same subject at different levels, the abler students have found a more steady challenge and less repetition. [Flexible Pacing for Able Learners, p. 97]

Explanation:

This sentence, like sentence 14, is long. The comma after *levels* separates a long introductory phrase; it does not separate subject from verb.

16. Junior college commissioner Dr. Lawrence Keating has announced a capital campaign county-wide to run from September, 1991, through May, 1992.

17. This trend, resulting in a 3% increase in sales for the third quarter, is expected to continue for at least two years.

18. John Elliot, my former teacher, has bought a home in your neighborhood.

Punctuation Beyond the Essentials

17–19. Use a colon to cast forward, a dash to cast back, and a semicolon to manage main clauses and complex series.

1. The next few pages describe an investment that we believe embodies these objectives: an investment that

combines income with tax benefits, that has historically performed well, that will fit in comfortably with
your present investment portfolio—an investment that
exhibits real potential to increase in value.

Explanation:

   This sentence in an investment brochure has a
colon after *objectives* because the series of statements
about the investment is intended to provide the objectives. In editing the sentence, I am bothered by the
departure from strict parallel structure. *An investment*
is repeated in the first element of the series and again
in the last element of the series, but not in the two
intermediate elements. I have used a dash to set off
the final element in the series, treating it as a departure from the rest of the series, and I have changed
which to *that*.

2. In her essay "In Search of Our Mothers' Gardens,"
   Alice Walker includes contrasting emotional tones:
   outrage balanced by sympathy, reverence set against
   disgust.

   Explanation:

   The colon separating *includes* from its objects is a
   violation of good form. I have chosen to move *contrasting emotional tones* in front of the colon, to provide an
   object for *includes*, and leave the two balanced phrases
   as they are, renaming tones.

3. What they fear is what most people want: a secure home,
   a regular schedule, rules that have some meaning.

   Explanation:

   Some writers feel uncomfortable using a series without a conjunction before the last element. The device is
   in wide use, however, and is generally accepted.

4. On his return to Paris in 1822, two years before his untimely death, Géricault produced some of his finest and
   most influential pictures: the group of drawings, lithographs, and watercolors of race and work horses and an

unforgettable series of realistic, haunting portraits of insane people. [Modern Prints and Drawings, p. 8]

Explanation:

In the original sentence the author included both a colon and a dash after *pictures*. Modern punctuation conventions will not permit both, and the colon makes better sense to me than the dash. The series that follows the colon is in fact a pair of noun phrases, each with internal commas. I am tempted to place a semicolon after *horses*, but to do so would be a departure from current conventions governing the use of the semicolon.

5. Why are the business applications of graphics growing so fast? There are two main reasons: lower hardware and software prices and the advances in computer graphics technology.

6. To drive out of the beleaguered city into the suburbs is immediately to encounter a different, happier world: a prosperous middle-class place that knows no violence—big comfortable houses built to sustain and celebrate the simple happiness of family life. [Sins and All, p 1.]

Explanation:

Editing for punctuation offers the opportunity to make the two verb forms parallel: *to drive . . . to encounter*. The writer used a semicolon after *violence* to indicate a break in the appositive phrase following and renaming *world*. The more conventional way of indicating such a break is with a dash. A comma would probably be enough.

7. Life leads us at a certain moment to step beyond the dualisms to which we have been educated: primitive and civilized, chaos and order, abnormal and normal, private and public, verbal and nonverbal, conventional and far-out, good and bad.

8. This guide is for people in industry who regularly write reports and proposals, memos and business letters.

They are counselors and architects, public administrators, surveyors, lawyers, and commercial artists—professionals who must communicate with clients and associates clearly and directly. [Guide, p. 5]

Explanation:

Notice that the dash points backward; *professionals* sums up the categories named before the dash.

9. The hardest part—this was no picnic, I assure you—was rechecking each address to be sure that no client had been listed incorrectly.

10. In practical terms, the scoring depends on the disposition of the judges—and that says it all.

11. The author regards this as typical adolescent behavior; however, I think the young woman is justified in feeling abandoned.

12. First of all, Virginia Woolfe's essay, "Professions for Women," gives the reader a sense of hearing the author in person, not just reading from a page.

13. Elsewhere honesty may be the best policy; in research it is the only policy.

14. Stated topic sentences often appear somewhere near the beginning of a paragraph, as in the first paragraph of this chapter; they can also appear at the end or even in the middle of a paragraph. [Writing for the Twenty-first Century, p. 162]

15. My grades were as follows: two A's, in economics and history; two B's, in accounting and chemistry; and a C in my only elective, History of Dance.

Explanation:

The reasons for the colon and the semicolons should be clear enough. The commas following *two A's* and *two B's* make clear that the speaker did not receive two grades in each subject.

Purely Conventional Punctuation

Refer to guidelines 20–24.

1. The man's attitude toward sex roles comes right out of "Genesis."

2. The female's lighter skeleton and her muscle structure suit her better than a man for some athletic activities.

3. Next summer Dr. White will offer his new course, "Artist of the Century": Picasso and Twentieth-Century Art. It will focus on our century's most influential artist.

   Explanation:

   No convention tells us how to punctuate the title of a course. In most college catalogues no quotation marks or italics set off the titles. The quotation marks in this course title are to identify *Artist of the Century* as an epithet for Picasso.

4. Exhibit 50, a survey of shipments during November, 1989, shows the shipper and location; the number of loads for each shipper; and whether each load was delivered "on time," "late," or "unknown."

   Explanation:

   Commas are needed to set off the restrictive phrase following *Exhibit 50*. I have deleted *which is*, in accordance with guideline 7e. I have supplied *each* in front of *load* because the loads would logically be identified separately. Semicolons separate the elements in the main series because the last element is itself a series with internal commas.

5. All this makes Judith seem more like an actual person and makes it easier to sympathize and to respond emotionally to what she suffers. We feel just how

unjust it is and how tragic for such a gifted young woman (or any young woman) to come to such a fate.

Explanation:

The colon after *suffers* could be replaced with a semicolon. I felt dividing the sentence into two would make the reading easier. I have removed the quotation marks from *gifted*. If Judith is not gifted, but simply called gifted, the context would justify the quotation marks. I have left the parenthetical phrase intact. A pair of dashes or commas would set off the phrase; the writer must judge how parenthetical the phrase is.

6. Several lineages of the earliest humanlike primates had evolved by about five million years ago. Among them were two Australopithecines ("southern apes"): the large *Australopithecus robustus* and the much smaller *Australopithecus africanus*. [Humankind, p. 40]

Explanation:

This passage tests the writer's knowledge of the labeling of species. *Australopithecines* is the Anglicized form of the Latin noun. Because it is English, it is in ordinary Roman type. *Southern apes* provides a more familiar English label for the species and is therefore in quotation marks. The final terms, *Australopithecus robustus* and *Australopithecus africanus,* are the Latin names and must be italicized. It is worth noting that *africanus* is not capitalized in Latin although its English cognate *African* would be.

7. On May 5, 1992, a major fund raising drive was launched in Austin, Texas, at the university law school.

8. That was the situation when the council began its campaign with the slogan, "Pick up with pride."

9. The magazine *Aura* is running a series of articles on the woman of the 90s as perceived by business leaders in the community.

Explanation:

Most writers would not treat *'90s* as a contraction of *1990s.*

10. "I am a little bit of a woman," Harriet Beecher Stowe wrote of herself in 1853, "somewhat more than 40, about as thin and dry as a piece of snuff." [Life, Special Report, p. 37]

Combining Punctuation Marks

By this point it should be well established that correct punctuation offers a range of possibilities for most sentences. There is no right way to punctuate a passage. The passages in this exercise are, with one exception, *paragraphs from books*. I will provide the punctuation that was in the originals. If the original punctuation differs from your punctuation, it is not necessarily better. Consider the punctuation intended by the author as one possibility.

1. Rarely in recent memory have people been faced with so much uncertainty when attempting to develop a successful investment strategy. The unsettled state of the economy, the enormous impact of taxes, the disarray of the Social Security system, and the distressing lack of consensus among experts as to which direction the economy is actually headed, raise serious questions about relying on traditional forms of investment. For investors seeking income, the bewildering and ever-changing number of investment choices—money market funds, bank certificates, savings and loan accounts, bonds, dividend-paying stocks—only add to the confusion. Where can individuals turn? Which investments make the most sense today? What should you look for in the income investments you choose? [QUIP II investment brochure]

2. My friends generally dropped out of school. Many of them, close during my elementary school years, no longer have an academic future; [they] simply refused the challenge and accepted the ways of the street. I saw this as losing at the game we all must play, a

game of chance [at which] only those with extra-ordinary determination can be successful. [Student paper]

Explanation:

This student example could not be corrected with punctuation alone. I have added some words, enclosed in brackets, to clarify the syntax. In rewriting the final sentence I have moved *at* so that the sentence does not end with a preposition. I do not take the position that it is an error to end a sentence with a preposition; I have moved the preposition to make the final clause stronger.

3. What I want to say is that as our personal universes expand, if we keep drawing ourselves into center *again and again*, everything seems to enhance everything else. It becomes unnecessary to choose which person to be as we open and close the same ball of clay. We will make pots for our English classes. Read poems to our pottery classes. Write on the clay, print from the clay. The activity seems to spring out of the same source: poem or pot, loaf of bread, letter to a friend, a morning's meditation, a walk in the woods, turning the compost pile, knitting a pair of shoes, weeping with pain, fainting with discouragement, burning with shame, trembling with indecision: what's the difference. I like especially two famous Zen stories: the one about the great Japanese master of the art of archery who had never in his life hit the bull's eye. And the other about the monk who said, "Now that I'm enlightened, I'm just as miserable as ever." [Centering, p. 23]

Explanation:

The author of this passage punctuates in unconventional ways. The most striking example is the long sentence in the middle of the paragraph, containing an extended series that begins and ends with colons. Notice, this long sentence is extended with a question but ends in a period, not a question mark. I include this example not to encourage unorthodox punctuation but to illustrate the lattitude published writing allows.

4. I want to repeat that this book is a guide, not a set of rules. If you find that following a guideline would make your writing sound unnatural, ignore the guideline. For example, the guide suggests you avoid passive constructions. Yet in some situations the passive sounds right. If it sounds right, it probably is. In the final analysis, the best writing sounds natural. One purpose behind these guidelines is to help you train your ear so that crisp, tight prose will sound right. The other purpose is to encourage you to trust your own judgment. [Guide, p. 5]

5. The town of Lake Wobegon, Minnesota, lies on the shore against Adams Hill, looking east across the blue-green water to the dark woods. From the south, the highway aims for the lake, bends hard left by the magnificent Grecian grain silos, and eases over a leg of the hill past the SLOW CHILDREN sign, bringing the traveler in on Main Street toward the town's one traffic light, which is almost always green. Along the ragged dirt path between the asphalt and the grass, a child slowly walks to Ralph's Grocery, kicking an asphalt chunk ahead of him. It is a chunk that after four blocks he is now mesmerized by, to which he is completely dedicated. At Bunsen Motors, the sidewalk begins. A breeze off the lake brings a sweet air of mud and rotting wood, a slight fishy smell, and picks up the sweetness of the old grease, a sharp whiff of gasoline, fresh tires, spring dust, and, from across the street, the faint essence of tuna hotdish from the Chatterbox Cafe. [Lake Wobegone Days, pp. 1–2]

Explanation:

The punctuation is that of Garrison Keillor. In this paragraph a construction with a preposition at the end—of a clause, not of a sentence—sounds perfectly natural to the author. It sounds okay to me, too. You may not have the typographic option of small lower-case letters to set off the phrase *slow children*. Any typographic variation would work: italics, underlining, quotation marks.

CHAPTER FOUR: AVOIDING SEXIST LANGUAGE

The paragraphs numbered 1 through 4 are long and require many changes. No single version will seem right to every reader. I have therefore not provided sample revisions. I urge you to follow the advice of your instructor or to share your revisions with others using this book. You may discover that your discussion of these passages will range far away from choosing the right language.

Refer to guidelines 25–30.

5. Short examples:

a. A good carpenter knows his tools and keeps them clean, sharp, and ready for use.

Correction:

   Good carpenters know their tools and keep them clean, sharp, and ready for use.

Alternate correction:

   A good carpenter knows tools and keeps them clean, sharp, and ready for use.

Explanation:

   If the context makes the singular form preferable to the plural, it is necessary to change the sense of the sentence slightly. The alternative is to use *his or her* before tools. This alternative is clumsy but better than using exclusive language.

b. Each passenger is responsible for his own luggage. He should have each bag or package tagged with his name and address.

Correction:

Passengers are responsible for their own luggage. They should have each bag or package tagged with name and address.

Alternate correction:

You are responsible for your own luggage. You should have each bag or package tagged with your name and address.

Explanation:

The first correction introduces a complicated agreement problem. The passengers are treated as plural, and yet each bag or package bears only one name and address. Treating *name* and *address* as abstractions without the possessive determiner solves the agreement problem but makes the sentence sound unreasonably formal. The alternate correction assumes the original sentences are instructions to passengers. If they are, it makes sense to address the passengers in the second person.

c. Anyone who wants his paper returned should include a self-addressed, stamped envelope.

Correction:

Anyone who wants this paper returned should include a self-addressed, stamped envelope.

Alternate correction:

If you want your paper returned, include a self-addressed, stamped envelope.

d. A good letter writer crafts the opening of a letter carefully, aware that a good impression begins with the first sentence. He doesn't spin his wheels.

He never starts with a word that ends in "ing":

Referring . . .

Replying . . .

He never starts with a phrase that ends with the preposition "to":

With reference to . . .

In answer to . . .

Pursuant to . . .

He never starts with a redundant expression:

I am writing . . .

For your information . . .

This is to inform you . . .

The purpose of this letter is . . .

We have received your letter . . .

Enclosed please find . . .

Attached herewith . . .

[adapted from a textbook on technical writing]

Correction:

Craft the opening of a letter carefully. Be aware that a good impression begins with the first sentence. Don't spin your wheels.

Never start with a word that ends in "ing":

Referring . . .

Replying . . .

Never start with a phrase that ends with the preposition "to":

With reference to . . .

In answer to . . .

Pursuant to . . .

Never start with a redundant expression:

I am writing . . .

For your information . . .

This is to inform you . . .

The purpose of this letter is . . .

We have received your letter . . .

Enclosed please find . . .

Attached herewith . . .

Explanation:

The shift to the imperative form makes these instructions more direct and more forceful. (By the way, this passage provides excellent advice for letter writers, particularly those in business.)

e. The artist's job in the beginning is not unlike the job of a writer. He or she must first reach out for raw material. He or she must spend much time making contact with actual objects. He or she must learn to see—to see correctly—using as many of the five senses as can reach through the eye at one time. [Adapted from The Natural Way to Draw, p. 5]

Correction:

In the beginning your job as an artist is not unlike the job of a writer. You must first reach out for raw material. You must spend much time making contact with actual objects. You must learn to see—to see correctly—using as many of the five senses as can reach through the eye at one time.

Explanation:

The adapted original, you might guess, was deliberately made clumsy by replacing *he* with *he or she*. The corrected version avoids the awkwardness of *he or she* by recasting the passage as instructions to the artist. Unfortunately, if the writer or editor adopted this revision of a dated book, the writer would then have to go through the whole book, changing the method of addressing its readers. The cost of revising to avoid sexist language can be high; it is better to use inclusive language in the first draft.

Glossary

This glossary presents definitions and explanations for most of the technical terms used in this book. The first time they appear in the body of the text the terms are printed in **boldface** type. The page numbers in parentheses identify the page where the term first appears in the text. The glossary is not intended as a grammar manual. Only terms necessary for understanding this book are included, and many definitions are incomplete, including only enough information to explain how the terms are used in this instance. Some terms are included to clarify the glossary but are not treated in the text.

abstract nominalization (14): See nominalization.

active (17): See voice.

adjectival (67): See adjective.

adjective (68): A word that modifies a noun or a noun phrase. The adjective form, adjectival, is used for phrases or other words that function as adjectives.

adverb (31): By its strictest definition an adverb modifies a verb. The term, often in its adjective form, adverbial, is used for a wide range of words, including conjunctive adverbs, other transition words, and intensifying words, not easily classified using traditional parts of speech.

adverbial modifier (75): See adverb; modifier.

adverbial (68): See adverb.

antecedent (65): See referent.

appositive (100): One of the uses for nouns. A noun is said to be an appositive, or in apposition, when it follows another noun that it renames or modifies. **Appositives** are treated as parenthetical additions and are set off by commas.

case (61): A grammatical category that identifies the forms of a noun or a pronoun, which in turn is based on how the noun or pronoun is used. The cases of English nouns are the subject case (nominative), the object case (objective), and the possessive case (genitive). The three cases are clearly distinguished only in pronouns: *I, he, she, they, who,* subject; *me, him, her, them, whom,* object; *my, mine, his, her, their, whose,* and so on, possessive.

clause (68): A clause is distinct from a phrase in that a clause has a subject and a finite verb. A clause is independent (a main clause) if it can stand alone as a sentence. A clause is dependent (a subordinate clause) if it is not complete in itself.

conjunction (72): A word that links words, phrases, clauses, or sentences. Coordinating conjunctions (*and, but, or, nor, for*) link units of equal grammatical or rhetorical status. Subordinating conjunctions (*although, when, if, because,* and the like) make one grammatical unit dependent on or subordinate to another.

conjunctive adverb (99): Sometimes classed as adverbs, these transition words link clauses in nearly the same way conjunctions do. A conjunctive adverb indicates a relationship between clauses, but does not subordinate the clause it introduces. Typical conjunctive adverbs: *however, nevertheless, moreover, consequently, therefore.*

coordinating conjunction (92): See conjunction.

count noun (56): A noun that can be counted and therefore has a plural form.

dangling modifier (58): Any word or group of words intended as a modifier that has no referent or word to modify, or a modifier so remote from the word it logically modifies that the relationship is not clear.

declarative sentence (86): A declarative sentence, punctuated at the end with a period, makes a statement. A declarative sentence is distinguished from an interrogative sentence, which poses a question and ends with a question mark, and an exclamatory sentence, which makes an emotional statement or expresses surprise and ends with an exclamation point.

dependent clause (72): See clause.

expletive (22): In the lexicon of grammar, an expletive is a word that fills a slot or takes the place of something else. The two common expletives in English are *there* (*there are sixteen stairs between the first floor and the landing*) and *it* (*it is difficult to drive on a narrow road*). In each sample sentence, the grammatical subject, displaced by the expletive, follows the verb.

finite verb (75): A verb that predicates or states the action of a clause. The main verb of a clause must be a finite verb. A finite verb is distinguished from the nonfinite verb forms: infinitives, gerunds, and participles.

first person (25): See person.

genitive case (110): Roughly equivalent to the possessive form, the genitive case is usually marked with '*s*. The genitive can be conveyed by using the preposition *of,* as in *the daughter of my friend,* or by simple position, as in *the Chicago area.* The genitive relationship is not confined to the possessive. *The boy's picture* may refer to a picture that belongs to the boy (possessive) or it may refer to a picture that portrays the boy.

gerund (145): A nonfinite verb form marked with -*ing* and used as a noun. In *The children enjoy singing, singing* is a gerund, used as the object of *enjoy.*

indefinite pronoun (56): A class of pronouns referring to unspecified referents. The simplest way to identify indefinite pronouns is to learn a list. *Anything, everyone, somebody, none, most,* and *some* are representative examples.

independent clause (72): See clause.

infinitive (150): A nonfinite verb form usually marked by *to*, as in *to ring, to dance, to talk*. Technically the infinitive form does not require *to*. In the sentence, *Visitors must register at the gate, register* is an infinite form, part of the verb phrase.

intensifying words (36): Typically regarded as adverbs, these modifiers are intended to strengthen the meanings of adjectives. Examples: *very, extremely, definitely, positively, absolutely*.

main clause (59): See clause.

mass noun (56): A noun that is normally not counted and therefore has no plural form (water, sand, air).

misplaced modifier (58): A modifier that is vague or confusing because it is not placed close enough to the word it is intended to modify.

modifier (58): The grammatical meanings of *modify* and *modifier* are nearly impossible to put into words. It is more helpful to say that adjectives modify nouns, adverbs modify verbs.

nominalization (14): A noun made from some other part of speech, most often from a verb. *Complication* is a nominalization (noun) made from the verb *complicate*. *Assessment* is derived from the verb *assess*. Because nominalizations are typically made from verbs, they refer to abstract actions (*comprehension, adherence*) rather than to concrete objects (*house, stone, person*). This book recommends avoiding abstract nominalizations.

nominative form (63): The form that identifies the subject of a clause or phrase. The nominative form is not restricted to the subject of a clause or sentence; an appositive or a noun following the linking verb *be* is in the nominative form.

nonrestrictive clause (37): An adjective clause that provides additional information about the noun it modifies, information not needed to identify the noun.

noun adjunct (71): A noun preceding another noun and modifying the second noun. In the phrase *a brick wall,* the first noun, *brick,* is a noun adjunct. In *government office, government* is a noun adjunct. The distinction between a noun adjunct and a genitive noun marked by its position is not always easy to establish.

noun phrase (57): A noun phrase is a group of words, syntactically related, that function as a single unit in any of the uses for nouns: subject, appositive, object or complement of the verb, object of a preposition.

object form (61): A function of case, the object form shows up only in pronouns. Examples: *me, us, him, her, them, whom.*

object (61): A grammatical function of nouns. Nouns may be objects of verbs or objects of prepositions.

parallel structure (68): The similarity in form that links coordinate words and phrases and helps to establish that they have a similar function. In the sentence *To learn is to grow,* the verbs, both infinitives, have parallel structure.

participial (59): See participle.

participle (59): A nonfinite verb used as an adjective, in its active or present form marked with *-ing.* Example: *The geese flying south pass over our farm in October. Flying* is a participle modifying *geese.* A passive or past participle is marked with *-ed,* if it is a regular verb, or has a distinctive past participle form. Example: *A picture drawn and colored by my daughter hangs on the bedroom door.* The participles are *drawn* and *colored.* The adjective form of *participle* is *participial.*

passive (14): See voice.

person (24): Personal pronouns are classified as first person (*I* and *we*), second person (*you*), or third person (*he, she, it, they*), depending on whether the pronouns refer to (1) the person or persons speaking, (2) the person or persons spoken to, or (3) the person or persons (or things) spoken about.

phrase (68): Any group of syntactically related words, distinguished from a clause because it does not contain a subject and a finite verb.

plural (55): We use *plural* to identify nouns or pronouns that refer to more than one entity. We use the same label for verbs when the subject of the verb is plural. The rule of agreement in English is that singular subjects require singular verbs, plural subjects require plural verbs.

possessive (70): The case formed by adding *'s* to most nouns. The possessive forms of pronouns are either modifying forms, *my, our, your, his, her, its, their,* or simple pronouns, *mine, ours, yours, his, hers, its, theirs. Whose* is the same in either use.

predicate (noun) (101): In most sentences the predicate can be identified as the main verb. Every sentence or clause must have a subject (doer) and a predicate (action). The predicate makes the main assertion of a sentence or clause. It must be a finite verb.

predicate (verb) (75): The main verb of a clause is said to predicate; that is, it states the action.

preposition (62): See prepositional phrase.

prepositional phrase (19): A prepositional phrase consists of a preposition and its object. *Under the door* is made up of the preposition *under* and an object, *the door.* The category of prepositions is best explained by a list: *under, over, around, beside, after, before, through.* When a word of this class is followed by a noun or noun phrase, as in *after the long summer,* the group of words is called a prepositional phrase.

pronoun (56): A word used in place of a noun or referring to an entity that might be labeled with a noun. This class of words includes personal pronouns, those identified as first person, second person, or third person, as well as the pronouns classed as indefinite pronouns and reflexive pronouns.

referent (antecedent) (63): Strictly speaking, a referent is whatever any word refers to. The term is most commonly used to identify the antecedent of a pronoun, that is, the word to which the pronoun refers.

reflexive (66): The reflexive form of a pronoun if formed by adding *-self* or *-selves* to the object or possessive form of the pronoun. The forms: *myself, ourselves, yourself, yourselves, himself, herself, itself, themselves.*

relative clause (37): A subordinate clause used as an adjective, introduced by a relative word, usually *who, which,* or *that.*

restrictive clause (37): An adjective clause that provides identifying information about the noun it modifies, information essential to make the sentence clear.

second person (24): See person.

sentence modifier (75): Typically adverbial in form (*frankly, truly*) or recognizable as a conjunctive adverb, a sentence modifier performs either of two functions. It may indicate the relation between the clause or sentence it modifies and another sentence (*therefore, however, nevertheless*), or it may identify the purpose, tone, or rhetorical intention of the speaker of the sentence (*frankly, honestly, hopefully, in truth*).

singular (55): We use *singular* to identify nouns and pronouns, or the verbs that agree with them, when these words refer to single entities. For the contrasting category, see plural.

subject (55): The doer of the action in a sentence or the topic of a sentence or clause. Every sentence or clause must have a subject (doer) and a predicate (action).

subordinate clause (69): See clause.

subordinating conjunction (72): See conjunction.

superlative (36): Adjectives and adverbs can be altered (inflected) to make them comparative (*bigger, fuller, faster, greener*) or superlative (*biggest, fullest, fastest,* *greenest*). Another way to make such words comparative or superlative is by modifying them with *more* or *most*.

syntax (68): The part of grammar that has to do with the relations between words, as opposed to the forms of words or their sounds.

tense (25): That quality of a verb, expressed in the form of the verb, that indicates the time of the verb: present, past, or future. Technically, English has only two verb tenses, present (*the plane arrives at noon*) and past (*the package arrived yesterday*). Informally we use *tense* to refer to any indication of time expressed in a verb phrase, such as future (*the morning will come*), perfect (*the flowers have bloomed*), or past progressive (*the dogs were barking*).

third person (24): See person.

transition words (28): Although it does not refer to a formal part of speech, this term includes coordinating conjunctions and subordinating conjunctions as well as conjunctive adverbs (*however, nevertheless, moreover,* and others). Transition words show the relations between words, phrases, or ideas.

voice (14): Verbs are either active or passive, depending on whether the action of the verb is performed by the subject on a grammatical object or whether the verb acts on the grammatical subject. *The building was constructed by a contractor.* This sentence is passive, its verb in the passive voice, because the subject, *building,* receives the action, *was constructed.* The sentence could be recast in the active voice: *A contractor constructed the building.* In general a strong, clear style favors the active voice and avoids passive constructions.

References

WRITING RESOURCES

This list of resources, stringently selective, includes the books I have found helpful for developing a simple, direct style. Although quite different in their approaches, these texts share a commitment to avoiding the offenses of bureaucratic style. I have not included dictionaries, a thesaurus, or a handbook for grammar and usage. Such reference works have a different purpose than the books on this list. The choice of specialized reference works, dictionaries of medical and legal terms for example, must be left to the individual because they are based on the writing needs of a particular profession or discipline. Style manuals covering the conventions of scholarly writing and the forms of citation and reference are available for various disciplines.

Barzun, Jacques. *Simple and Direct: A Rhetoric for Writers.* Rev ed. New York: Harper & Row, 1985.

Christensen, Francis, and Bonniejean Christensen. *A New Rhetoric.* New York: Harper & Row, 1976.

Cook, Claire Kehrwald. *Line by Line: How to Improve Your Own Writing.* Boston: Houghton Mifflin, 1986.

Frank, Francine Wattman, and Paula A. Treichler. *Language, Gender, and Professional Writing: Theoretical Approaches and Guidelines for Nonsexist Usage.* New York: Modern Language Association, 1989.

Gibson, Walker. *Tough, Sweet and Stuffy: An Essay on Modern American Prose Styles.* Bloomington: Indiana University Press, 1966.

Lanham, Richard A. *Revising Business Prose.* New York: Macmillan, 1987.

Strunk, William, Jr. *The Elements of Style.* With Revisions, an Introduction, and a Chapter on Writing by E. B. White. (1959) 3rd ed. New York: Macmillan, 1979.

Trimble, John R. *Writing with Style: Conversations on the Art of Writing.* Englewood Cliffs, NJ: Prentice-Hall, 1975.

Weathers, Winston. *An Alternate Style: Options in Composition.* Rochelle Park, NJ: Hayden Book Company, 1980.

Williams, Joseph M. *Style: Ten Lessons in Clarity and Grace.* 2nd ed. Glenview, IL: Scott, Foresman, 1985.

Zinsser, William. *On Writing Well: An Informal Guide to Writing Nonfiction.* (1979) 2nd ed. New York: Harper & Row, 1980.

WORKS CITED

This list provides bibliographical information for works cited in the guide, including some passages used in the exercises. Because I often comment on the style of the text, including punctuation, type face, and other variables, the references are not necessarily to the most current or authoritative edition of each source.

American Psychology Association. *Publication Manual of the American Psychological Association.* 3rd ed. Washington, D.C.: American Psychology Association, 1983.

Connors, J. Robert, and Andrea A. Lunsford. "Frequency of Formal Errors in Current College Writing, or Ma and Pa Kettle Do Research." *College Composition and Communication* 39 (1988): 395–409.

Farb, Peter. *Humankind.* (Houghton Mifflin, 1978) New York: Bantam, 1980.

Fowler, H. W. *A Dictionary of Modern English Usage*. 2nd ed., rev. by Ernest Gowers. New York: Oxford University Press, 1965.

Gould, Stephen Jay. *Wonderful Life: The Burgess Shale and the Nature of History*. New York: Norton, 1989.

Hairston, Maxine. "Not All Errors Are Created Equal: Non-academic Readers in the Professions Respond to Lapses in Usage." *College English* 43 (1981): 794–806.

Hartwell, Patrick. "Grammar, Grammars, and the Teaching of English." *College English* 47 (1985): 105–127.

National Council of Teachers of English. *Guidelines for Non-sexist Use of Language in NCTE Publications*. Urbana, IL: National Council of Teachers of English, 1985.

Thomas, Lewis. *The Medusa and the Snail: More Notes of a Biology Watcher*. Toronto and New York: Bantam, 1980.

White, E. B. *Letters of E. B. White*. Col. and ed. by Dorothy Lobrano Guth. New York: Harper Colophon, 1978.

SOURCES

The following are sources for sample sentences and paragraphs, used throughout the book.

Barzun, Jacques, and Henry F. Graff. *The Modern Researcher*. 3rd ed. San Diego: Harcourt Brace Jovanovich, 1977.

Blicq, Ron. *Technically Write—Communicating in a Technological Era*. 2nd ed. Englewood Cliffs, NJ: Prentice Hall, 1981.

Borden Publishing Company. *The Drawings of Picasso*. Introduction by Arthur Millier. Los Angeles: Borden, 1961.

Christensen, Francis, and Bonniejean Christensen. *Notes toward a New Rhetoric: Nine Essays for Teachers*. 2nd ed. New York: Harper & Row, 1978.

Daniel, Neil, and June Cox. *Flexible Pacing for Able Learners*. ERIC Clearinghouse on Handicapped and Gifted Children. Reston, VA: Council for Exceptional Children, 1988.

Farb, Peter. *Humankind*. New York: Bantam, 1980.

Freeman, Joan. "The IQ as a Measure of Intellectual Giftedness." *Face to Face with Giftedness*. Ed. Bruce M. Shore, Françoys Gagné, Serge Larivée, Richard E. Tremblay. New York: Trillium Press, 1983.

Gould, Stephen Jay. *The Panda's Thumb: More Reflections in Natural History*. New York and London: Norton, 1982.

Irwin, Howard S. *Roadside Flowers of Texas*. The Elma Dill Russell Spencer Foundation Series 1. Austin: University of Texas Press, 1961.

Jacquard, Albert. "Highly Gifted, or People?" *Face to Face with Giftedness*. Ed. Bruce M. Shore, Françoys Gagné, Serge Larivée, Richard E. Tremblay. New York: Trillium Press, 1983.

Johanson, Donald, and James Shreeve. *Lucy's Child: The Discovery of a Human Ancestor*. New York: William Morrow, 1989.

Keillor, Garrison. *Lake Wobegon Days*. New York: Viking, 1985.

Kramer, Alan. "The Gifted Child as Freak: Brilliance as Handicap." *Face to Face with Giftedness*. Ed. Bruce M. Shore, Françoys Gagné, Serge Larivée, Richard E. Tremblay. New York: Trillium Press, 1983.

Krauter, William P. *A Guide to Achieving Style through Effective Writing*. Fort Worth, TX: General Dynamics, 1975.

Montgomery, Dave. "Meet the Press Secretary." *Fort Worth Star-Telegram* 19 Nov. 1989, section 5:1, 12–13.

Nicolaïdes, Kimon. *The Natural Way to Draw: A Working Plan for Art Study*. Boston: Houghton Mifflin, 1941.

"Noble Causes: Crusaders for the Sick, Poor and Oppressed." *Life Special Report: Remarkable American Women, 1776–1976*. New York: Time Inc.

Pratt & Whitney Aircraft. *General Operating Instructions: Dual Axial Compressor Afterburning Turbojet Engines.* East Hartford, CT: United Aircraft Corporation, 1957.

Prepare to Sell: A Recipe for Successful Selling. Life Insurance Agency Management Association, 1972.

QUIP II: Quinoco Oil and Gas Income Program II. Denver: Quinoco.

Richards, Mary Caroline. *Centering: In Pottery, Poetry, and the Person.* 1964. Middletown, CT: Wesleyan University Press, 1976.

Sachs, Paul J. *Modern Prints and Drawings: A Guide to a Better Understanding of Modern Draughtsmanship.* New York: Knopf, 1954.

Souerwine, Andrew H. *Career Strategies: Planning for Personal Achievement.* New York: Amacom, 1978.

Wilson, A. N. "C. S. Lewis, Sins and All." *New York Times Book Review.* 24 Dec. 1989, 1, 26–27.

Wresch, William, Donald Pattow, and James Gifford. *Writing for the Twenty-First Century: Computers and Research Writing.* New York: McGraw-Hill, 1988.